D0685117

CHARITY, MORALITY, SEX AND YOUNG PEOPLE

CHARITY, MORALITY, SEX AND YOUNG PEOPLE

FR. ROBERT J. FOX

240
FO

OUR SUNDAY VISITOR, INC.
HUNTINGTON, INDIANA

ISBN: 0-87973-763-8
Library of Congress Catalog Card Number: 74-21889

Cover Design by James E. McIlrath

Published, printed and bound in the U.S.A. by
Our Sunday Visitor, Inc.
Noll Plaza,
Huntington, Indiana 46750
763

Contents

PRAYER BEFORE STUDY

Jesus, Mary and Joseph, I take this book in my hands to study a sacred subject of God's own creation. Sex is sacred, so sacred that God has deigned to use its power in His act of creating new human beings and the condition upon which He creates new immortal souls to be happy with Him forever in heaven.

Whatever is so sacred is also capable of abuse and misrepresentation. Victim as I am to the consequences of Original Sin, darkened mind and weakened will, I ask you Holy Spirit, Spouse of the Virgin Mother, to enlighten my mind and strengthen my will so that I may more fully comprehend Your own divine plan in sharing with the human race your marvelous powers of life-giving and love-giving. If I can behold your marvelous powers and purposes, Almighty God, working in Your creation, including that of human love blended with the divine, I shall behold only goodness and holiness all the days of my life and see that what You, dear God, have done is good.

Sacred Heart of Jesus, I desire to be touched by the fire of Your Love at once human and divine. Immaculate Heart of Mary, intercede for me that I may always be pure and know my true vocation in life according to God's will. St. Joseph, Guardian of Virgins and Protector of the Holy Family, intercede that I may come to the knowledge of the sanctity of family life.

Almighty God, give me a profound desire always to live in Your grace, indwelt by the most Blessed Trinity, a temple of God in body and soul. Amen.

FOREWORD

Young people have a right to be informed about sex. If you are a Catholic teenager or young adult, you have a right to know clearly the teachings of the Catholic Church on the morality of sex. You should not have to guess at what is right or wrong, at what is good and what is beautiful. I have written this book drawing from my experiences with good and honest inquiring Catholic young people during the years I've spent in Christ's holy priesthood.

I have learned that the average Catholic teenager wants to know the facts. He or she is not frightened when Catholic Christian morality seems challenging, even difficult at times. I've found that our Catholic young people love God very much and are grateful when they are spoken to honestly and feel that they can come to a priest, a parent, a counselor for spiritual guidance. They are not looking for the easiest course to take. Teenagers soon lose trust in the adult who communicates permissiveness. They do not want a permissive Christ but one who makes demands.

When necessary, teenagers will take up their cross and follow Jesus.

It is reassuring to the Catholic teenager, to the young man and young woman, to learn that he or she is not the only one with problems, with temptations. It is hopeful to learn that today's adults, among those who stand for a morality in Christ which is strict, challenging and demanding, themselves had to battle forces of evil and godless mentalities during their teen years. It is encouraging to know that others understand and can be forgiving of one's failures.

Studies show that the conservative Churches are holding their members and are growing. Pope Paul VI has said that the Catholic Church is "tenaciously conservative." He means it. "Conservative" is not a bad word. It means in the case of religion to *conserve* true faith and morality. Some have given a false image of the Catholic Church, its faith and morals. The Church is not in doubt about its faith or about its morals. This includes the morality of sex.

What about the kiss, the embrace, fornication, adultery, artificial birth control, abortion, masturbation, inter-personal relationships between adolescent boys and girls? When is sex holy? You know the questions. What are the answers? What is sinful? How far can one go? What is venial sin? What is mortal sin? What is no sin at all? More important, what is good, beautiful and the will of God? How can I know for certain about the morality of sex? If you think it important enough to find the answers without ambiguity, then you will peruse these pages carefully and completely.

CHAPTER I

SEX INVOLVES CHARITY AND LIFE — HUMAN AND DIVINE

I debated for considerable time about the title I should give this book. First, there was the question whether to use the word "love" in place of "charity." The two words, love and charity, mean essentially the same. I decided on the word "charity." Why? Because most people still know the meaning of the word "charity." Many do not know the real meaning of "love." Love, for many, has come to mean only sex. For still others, love can mean "permissiveness." People in authority who are permissive may fear they will not show concern if they are restrictive or demanding. Thus those under the charge of permissive authority may not rise to Christian challenges. The word "charity" fortunately still conveys the meaning of unselfishness, mercy, kindness, understanding, concern for others. Ultimately, charity is the overflow of God's love in our relationships with each other.

Another matter I debated in selecting the

title for this book was whether to place the adjective "Catholic" in front of the words "young people." I did not want to convey any idea that in God's plan there was any difference between sexual morality for Catholics and anyone else. What is sexually wrong for Catholics is wrong for everyone else, regardless of creed or nationality. Some others may not agree but that does not change the truth. For that matter there may even be *some* Catholics who will disagree with what they know is the teaching of Almighty God and His holy Church. But that does not make them right. Sin is sin by whatever other name some may choose to call it.

Still another decision I had to make in preparing this book on charity, morality, sex and young people was whether to prepare a separate book for boys and still another for girls. I recalled that past popes have favored individualized and separate instruction on the subject. After all, God did make boys and girls differently while making both of them in His own image and likeness. But young people often find themselves with many problems precisely because they have not sufficiently understood the opposite sex. Boys and girls can help one another develop while remaining pure if they better understand one another. While popes and prudent teachers of religion may well propose separate instructions on sex for boys and for girls, they do not propose ignorance of, shall we say, "the complementary sex" rather than the "opposite sex." Surely it would not be proper to discuss detailed biological differences and problems in detail in mixed classrooms. For the most part, this book should be studied in private, preferably under the guidance of one's father or mother, a parish priest or religious or CCD teacher. Hopefully, the study of the contents will lead to discussion, where necessary, with one's parents, a confessor or spiritual director.

The discussion questions at the end of each chapter could well be used in mixed groups, in religion classrooms, if discussed with the Christian dignity and reverence, I am confident, our young people desire regarding human sexuality.

In my work as a parish priest, teacher, journalist and lecturer, I have come to realize the very great need for instruction in this area. I remember well my own teen years. How grateful I shall always be that I was led to excellent instruction by holy priests and religious. I had the privilege as a teenager to meet a famous Jesuit priest who had a way with youth. His name was Father Daniel A. Lord. He spoke and wrote bluntly but reverently. His writings and speeches sank deeply into my mind, filling my soul with the love of God, the beauty of truth and purity, and the real place of sex in God's plan. Some of these very thoughts, planted in my mind long ago by such holy priests, may now bud forth again to blossom in other youthful souls.

What has concerned me and countless numbers of parents and priests I come into contact with across the country is the teaching of sex without morality. There are books available on sex, some of them hundreds of pages long, but with hardly a word on the morality of the right and wrong use of sex. Some of these books are being used not only in public schools but, sometimes, even in Catholic schools.

Before going any further in my visit with you young people, I should say this. The purpose of this book is *not* to point out the evil of sex. Sex is good. In the Bible at the dawn of creation when God created our first parents, Adam and Eve, God commanded that first man and woman to increase and multiply. When God, according to the Genesis account, beheld all that He had made, He saw that it was good. But when God had finally made man and woman in His own image and likeness, God saw "it was *very* good."

God created man in the image of himself, in the image of God he created him, God blessed them, saying to them, 'Be fruitful, multiply, fill the earth and conquer it . . .' God saw all he had made, and indeed it was very good" (Gn. 1:27-31).

God has given the human race the power of sex. It may be used in marriage to foster love between husband and wife and for the fruitfulness and multiplication of the human race of which God spoke. God could have chosen another means of bringing human life into the world after our first parents. He could have created each new human being by a separate act of creation. But God chose to involve husband and wife in each of His acts of creating new human life. God, so to speak, has tied His own hands. God will not create a new human being with an immortal soul unless husband and wife cooperate. Their act of love in marriage, when God so wills it, will bring forth new human life into which God fuses an immortal soul which will live forever. Husband and wife cooperate in God's highest act of creation, for man is little less than the angels. He is the highest of all God's creation in the universe we know.

Look at the new born babe. It is so precious. It has an immortal soul. That baby is a person. It is a person with a soul even before it is born. Modern science offers abundant evidence that there is human life from the moment of conception, even nine months before birth. This is why the Church teaches us that abortion at any stage is murder. A Catholic who would submit to or even assist in an abortion would be automatically excommunicated from the Church. Abortion is murder for everyone, be they Catholic, Protestant, Orthodox, Jew, or any of the various pagan religions, or no religion at all, because it is against God's law.

I can still remember vividly the missionary who came to my home parish when I was a youngster. He told the story of an expectant mother who went to the doctor to have her baby aborted. She had recently conceived. The doctor told the mother to come back in nine months. "Then I will wring its neck." The mother screamed and accused the doctor of being willing to commit murder. The doctor had made his point. He turned to the woman and bluntly stated, "And so are you willing to commit murder at this very moment. For that is what it would be right now, if I assisted you in an abortion."

Doctors, both Catholic and Protestant, have told me that as Christian doctors who have always dedicated their time and talent to saving and promoting human life, they would under no circumstances assist in murdering human life at any stage. I know of one town in rural America where there are five doctors. When the Black Monday of

January 22, 1973 saw the Supreme Court handing down its abortion decision, they quickly met and all five doctors, none of them Catholic, agreed that under no circumstances would they break their oath to respect and foster human life at every stage of development, beginning with the traditional nine months before birth.

What all of us must remember is this. What is legal is not necessarily morally right. The same is true of contraceptives. It may be legal for people to buy artificial birth control devices. It may be legal to practice artificial birth control. But that does not make it right before God. Abortion, however, is something even more serious. Artificial birth control, while morally wrong, does not involve the destruction of human life. It is the prevention of human life. Abortion is the *killing* of human life already conceived.

I have discussed these various topics to introduce you to the truth that sex ultimately is involved with human life, new life that is in God's own image and likeness. When something is sacred, the abuse of it is sinful. Sex is sacred. It is beautiful. It is part of God's act of creation. Its desecration makes us accountable before God because sex is so sacred. Never should love-giving and life-giving in sex be separated. Since only validly married people are permitted by God to co-operate with Him in life-giving, the love-giving which involves sex is reserved only to validly married people.

The Catholic young person must be prepared to meet today's godless concepts of sex. Even people who call themselves Christian, and some who call themselves "Catholic Christian" do not have an authentic Catholic or Christian mind on the sacredness of sex. Morality is not determined by votes or by the latest poll.

When it comes to the judgment, (and death is no respecter of age, scripture reminds us), our fellow man will not judge us. It will be God Himself. God established a Church in Jesus Christ. The Church is the Mystical Body of Jesus Christ. The Church speaks for Christ. Jesus promised the Church the Holy Spirit to keep it in the truth. Jesus tells us, and the Bible records, that when we listen to the Church we are listening to Jesus Himself. If we reject the Church, we are rejecting Jesus and therefore God the Father Who sent Jesus to this earth to establish the Church. Jesus built His Church upon Peter the Rock and said, "The gates of hell shall not prevail against it" (Mt. 16:18). The Catholic Church is the voice of Jesus, therefore of God, speaking to us today.

In this book on charity, morality, sex and young people, I shall present not opinions, but the voice of Jesus as presented by His Church. In a world in turmoil, in a sex-saturated society without morality, the purpose of this book will be to challenge young people to be generous, self-sacrificing, seeking to live their Catholic Christian lives fully and in harmony with the mind of Jesus Christ. This book is designed to help young people form their consciences *correctly*.

There is too much of the "conscience game" being played today. It is trickery. It is phoney morality. Some call it "situation ethics." Some present the conscience as supreme, disregard the teachings of God in scripture and in His holy Church and claim that they can form their consciences whichever way pleases them best. They forget that if we believe in Almighty God, if we believe His Son became man and founded the Church to carry on His work, we must form our consciences *correctly* by listening to Jesus in His Church.

QUESTIONS FOR DISCUSSION
1. How do some people misunderstand the word "love" today?
2. Give a Christian definition or explanation of love.
3. Does God have one standard of morality for Catholic Christians and another standard for other Christians and those of other beliefs?
4. Why should some aspects of sex education be differentiated or separated for boys and girls?
5. Why should sex *not* be considered or taught in isolation of Christian morality?
6. Why is sex in itself never to be considered evil?
7. When does human life begin to exist according to the almost universal agreement of scientists?
8. The Church imposes automatic *excommunication* on any Catholic who has or actively assists in an abortion. Why is abortion considered so serious by the Church?
9. What does the author mean by the "Conscience Game"?

It is suggested that youthful readers become well informed of the National *Right to Life* movement of concerned people. These people are determined to protect the right of the lives of the unborn as

well as be *pro-life* for all people already born.
Birthright is another valuable organization that
deserves respect. It works to assist frightened
young mothers, especially unwed mothers, who
might otherwise be tempted to seek the solution
to their problem in the abortive death of their unborn child. In gaining the advice of those willing
to help, witnessing the compassion and understanding of others prepared and experienced in
helping those with such serious problems, thousands of babies have thus been born to see the
light of day, to be washed in the sanctifying
waters of baptism, and given the right to a full life
of love and happiness in time and in eternity.

CASSETTE ON SEX EDUCATION
by FATHER FOX

No. 4   *Christian Youth and Sex Education*
by Father Robert J. Fox

A one-hour recording for presentation to teenagers, especially grades 7 through 12. Frank and reverent discussions
of the problems and temptations of boys and girls. The
beauty of purity is stressed in a conversational tone and
teenagers are encouraged to trust in the love of God and
make generous use of the sacraments. It will answer many
questions and help put young people in a more direct
touch with the author of this book. ($5.50 cassette; $6.50
reel.)

Order by number direct from:
POPE PUBLICATIONS: BOX 6161, SAN RAFAEL,
CALIFORNIA 94903

CHAPTER II

CHARITY AND MORALITY

"So there abide faith, hope and charity, these three; but the greatest of these is charity" (I Cor. 13:13). A good Christian life is not restricted to obeying the Sixth Commandment. But then I never heard anyone who said it was.

Despite what you may read and hear today, the Catholic Church was not all hung up on sex before Vatican Council II. On the contrary, the world today is saturated with it. One can hardly listen to a talk show without the subject being thrown in amidst immature giggles. And by adults. Commercials appeal to animal sex instincts as do magazine stories and pictures. I do not mean the sex instinct is entirely animal in man. It is just that too often a sex saturated society reduces it to that level. The *Playboy* approach is hardly an attempt to reach for the mature Christian values of womanhood and manhood.

One of the most commonly quoted sex experts whose efforts are dominating sex education programs today has said, "Sex is for fun." That is false. When sex is only for fun, it is immoral and against the plan of God. Sex in marriage, rightly exercised, is the highest expression of love between a Christian husband and wife. Sealed with the Sacrament of Matrimony, it is a means of worshiping God and growing in grace.

If sex were only for fun, then it would be permissible for anyone and everyone, everywhere. That godless thinking is more and more dominating the mentality of people today. Therefore we are exposed to unchristian thinking which permits premarital sex, partner switching among the married, divorce, abortion, artificial birth control, self abuse or masturbation. You Catholic young people must prepare yourselves to keep your minds and consciences Christ-like and correctly formed. You must be *different*.

How subtly the devil is working in society. Immorality passes for Christian love. You hear the thinking expressed in subtle ways. "It is OK to have sex before marriage if you really love the person and neither partner is hurt." *That is a lie.* It is contrary to God's Word in scripture and the official pronouncements of His holy Church.

A permissive, subtle, nebulous morality that lets you rather than God and His Church decide what is morally right and morally sinful may appear attractive, but in the long run, whenever anyone goes against God's plan (and His laws merely dictate His will for our happiness), unhappiness and the loss of peace will result. Tragedy enters the lives of those who habitually live contrary to God's laws. An increasing number of young adults today, having bought for a time a permissive new morality that was not based on truth, have ended in utter despair which led to suicide. Thousands of others have ruined their lives and deprived themselves the full measure of happiness God intended for them even in this world.

It would *not* be easier or bring greater happiness if the Church were to approve of the use of sex for fun outside of marriage, either privately or with another. God's holy laws upon which the Church bases her teachings in sexual morality stem from the very nature of truth, goodness, beauty, peace, order, happiness. Religious truth is truth. Truth based on God is immutable. God could never permit His Church to change truth.

Sometimes the expression "Natural Law" is used. This means rule or order that is rooted in the very nature of things. God created all things. He put order in His creation. God Himself is the Author of the laws of nature. If we go against nature we will have disorder, the lack of beauty and goodness. This will end in the lack of peace and in unhappiness. Nonrational creatures follow the natural law as they have no freedom to violate it. Man is the one creature of God with a free will to say *"No"* to God's plan. The Natural Law refers to what is *right* according to the very nature of things which God has created. Sex just for fun, separated from married love and from the natural exercises of love-giving and life-giving is wrong both from the viewpoint of the Natural Law and the positively expressed law of God and of His Church. St. Thomas Aquinas said: "Just as grace presupposes nature, the Divine Law presupposes the Natural Law."

Young people, please do not conclude that I am attempting to say that sex is not pleasurable. It is pleasurable both in marriage and outside of marriage. But out of order, out of place, it is seriously sinful and can bring unhappiness for others besides those who have committed the sin. In place, in marriage, it brings happiness and when fruitful in new human life, it spreads its happiness and goodness to others. This is because sex is then used and respected as sacred. Married people who use sex in an unnatural way, just for their own selfish pleasure without assuming the responsibility of giving life, have separated love-giving from life-giving. These couples ultimately experience frustration and unhappiness. This is one reason so many marriages today are ending in divorce.

God intended sex to be used only by a validly married husband and wife. Jesus raised such married love to the dignity of a sacrament whereby their unselfish sharing is sanctified in Christ. Their natural love is supernaturalized in the holy state of Matrimony. Sex is only a minor, if important, part of true marriage. *It is the expression of the total giving of husband and wife to each other in Christ.* The sexual embrace of husband and wife is merely a climactic expression of their love that is exercised all day, all week, all year long in caring for one another and the family. The daily cares of business, chores, nourishing and healing the family members, entertainment and recreation together as a family such as the family picnic, or games, meals, — all these are expressions of family love. Their love *in Christ* is expressed more directly at family prayer time, and participating in the holy Sacrifice of the Mass together as a family. All this is Christian family love. Husband and wife, in the embrace of married love that is private and exclusive to them alone in the family circle, express at that time a total giving of self to each other in the most pleasurable and expressive manner possible. Without the generous self sacrifice of work and charitable giving in other ways throughout the day, week and year, the sexual embrace would be meaningless and selfish.

God did attach a very great pleasure to the sexual embrace. There are various reasons for this. There is great sacrifice involved in rearing a family. A child brought into the world must be nursed and nourished for many years with great patience and generosity. God encourages husbands and wives to be generous by attaching an award of pleasurable love to their love-giving and live-giving. Every child conceived by an authentically Christian husband and wife is the fruit of love that is noble and pure. God made sex. Therefore it has to be holy. Only its abuse is sinful. Of all the disorder that entered our lives as a result of Original Sin, that disorder often evidenced in the sex appetite is most graphic.

I am not saying sex appetite is wrong. It is not wrong for boys and girls to be drawn toward each other. That is natural and good. But it can get out of control, dis-ordered. Then sin enters in. As a result of the consequences we inherit through Original Sin, our minds have been darkened and our wills weakened in some respects. It is not easy to keep our appetites, our passions under control. Baptism washes away Original Sin. Baptism gives Sanctifying Grace to our souls for the very first time. We then share in God's own life. But still, the consequences of Original Sin remain. Our human nature has been weakened. We must struggle to keep order in our lives. We need God's holy grace to strengthen us in our battle for what is good, true and beautiful.

Sometimes young people ask this question. "You say that sex before marriage is sinful, even mortally sinful. But suddenly after marriage, with a short marriage ceremony, the *same thing* is no longer sinful. Then you almost glorify it. You call it sacred and even a means of worshiping God and growing in grace. What gives here? You mean a piece of paper and a few words by a priest makes sin sacred?" The question is worth considering. It shows, however, a basic lack of understanding and appreciation of the very nature of sex and the plan of God.

It is not a piece of paper or the few words of the priest that changes the nature of sex outside of marriage from that within a valid Christian marriage. I say this even though *normally* in the case of a Catholic, a priest is required in the exchange of the marriage vows for the couple to be validly married before God and His holy Church.

Matrimony is one Sacrament the priest does not administer. The priest is merely an official witness required by the Church. The priest offers prayers, offers the holy Sacrifice of the Mass for the spiritual and temporal welfare of the newly created family. Jesus Christ placed the Church in charge of all seven sacraments. Therefore it is the responsibility of the Church to see that the couple desirous of entering into marriage are qualified, know their responsibilities and are determined to enter a *life-long commitment. If a couple attempted* marriage without the intention of "until death do us part" and if their intention to use sex in marriage would involve a plan for *permanent* and unnatural separation of love-giving from life-giving, their marriage would be invalid.

It is the man who administers the Sacrament of Matrimony to the woman. The woman administers the Sacrament of Matrimony to the man. We do not say, (or should not say) that the priest marries the couple. They marry each other. The priest is the official witness of the Church and normally where one or both are Catholics being married, the priest is required by Church law. Jesus gave His Church the power to make laws and said, "Whatsoever you bind upon earth, shall be bound in heaven." Therefore heaven respects the Church laws for the good of the couple's holiness and happiness.

The marriage ceremony, at which time the couple enter into a sacred contract with God and each other in Christ, is the *beginning* of their life-long commitment to each other in faith, hope and charity. Only when the Church, which has authority over Matrimony as over all the sacraments, approves of a couple as being prepared to enter that solemn life-long commitment, may they solemnly exchange their marriage vows and thus administer the sacrament to each other. The newly married couple, thus joined together in Christ have their marriage finally consummated and rendered indissoluble when they engage in their first sexual embrace. Before marriage the sexual embrace called intercourse would be not only seriously sinful, but a lie. God forbids it seriously. The Bible clearly states: fornicators shall not inherit the kingdom of heaven.

The Apostle St. Paul says in the Bible, "You know perfectly well that people who do wrong will not inherit the kingdom of God: people of immoral lives, idolaters, adulterers, catamites, sodomites, thieves, usurers, drunkards, slanderers and swindlers will never inherit the kingdom of God" (I Cor. 6:9-10). There are many places in the Bible where God is most clear that sex before marriage, or sex after marriage with someone not of one's marriage partner (adultery), is seriously sinful and deprives one of the right to heaven. There are no exceptions. Fornication and adultery are always sinful. "Keep away from fornication . . . to fornicate is to sin against your own body. Your body you know is the temple of the Holy Spirit. . . . You are not your own property . . ." (I Cor. 6:18-20).

There are absolutes in Christian morality. Absolutes mean no exceptions. The Catholic Church issued the *General Catechetical Directory* in 1971 to remind us of that very point among other matters of teaching authentic Catholic faith and morals. That *General Catechetical Directory* was not just an opinion but a presentation of the official Church position for the Church all over the world. The Supreme Pontiff, Pope Paul VI, approved this General Directory, confirmed it by his authority and ordered it to be published. I am quoting this authoritative document because it is essential that it be deeply impressed upon the minds and consciences of young Catholics that God does speak to us through our Pope.

"Christian freedom still needs to be

*ruled and directed in the concrete circum-
stances of human life. Accordingly, the conscience of the faithful, even when informed
by the virtue of prudence, must be subject to
the Magisterium of the Church, whose duty it
is to explain the whole moral law authorita-
tively, in order that it may rightly and correctly express the objective moral order"
(GCD 63).*

Before continuing to share with you this official position of the Catholic Church, let me explain that "Magisterium" means the teaching authority of the Chirch entrusted originally to the
Apostles with Peter as their head. Jesus promised
He would guide that Magisterium in *faith and
morals* through the power of the Holy Spirit, the
Spirit of Truth (Jn. 14:14-17, Jn. 15:26, Jn. 16:13).
The Magisterium, which is the voice of Jesus in
the Church, and will be such until the end of the
world (Mt. 16:18-20), now resides in our present
Holy Father, the Pope, who is the successor of St.
Peter. It also resides in the Bishops of the world
provided they speak together with and under the
successor of Peter.

An individual priest or even bishop may go
astray in teaching us true doctrines of faith or
morals. Even several such teachers could. The responsibility of each priest, bishop or any teacher
of religion in the Church when they speak on matters of faith or morals, is to communicate *only*
what is the authentic teaching on Catholic faith
and morals as made known by the Magisterium.
One bishop or several bishops are not the Magisterium. Any bishop speaking contrary to the Pope

is not promised the guidance of the Spirit of Truth.

The *General Catechetical Directory* continues.

> *"Further, the conscience itself of Christians must be taught that there are norms which are absolute, that is, which bind in every case and on all people. That is why the saints confessed Christ through the practice of heroic virtues; indeed, the martyrs suffered even torture and death rather than deny Christ" (GCD 63).*

So see then, how differently the Church speaks in Jesus' Name from those who would attempt to explain away sin. Some would say, in this particular case, impurity is not sin at all but rather love. They *falsely* say that these two young people love each other very much and God intended sex even for them to be a love act. They should therefore be able to express their love fully. The only limitation would be that they make a responsible and mutual decision and no one gets hurt. Such thinking is straight from hell. It is contrary to the Word of God in the Bible and contrary to the very clear teaching of the Church. The Church says this is an absolute norm binding everyone. *Fornication and adultery are always forbidden by God.* Even if we cannot understand all of God's reasons, God's authority should be enough to convince us, if we truly have faith in the God of love, beauty, order and truth.

In 1973 our own Catholic Bishops of the United States responded to Rome's *General Catechetical Directory* by issuing a document called *Basic*

Teachings for Catholic Religious Education. The highest Church authority in Rome subsequently approved of that document. I am telling you about these documents and quoting from them so that no one can say that the moral teachings of the Church are not clear. Our Bishops told us that we have specific duties and obligations flowing from the love of God and man.

> "Many are the sins against neighbor. It is sinful to be selfishly apathetic towards others in their needs. It is sinful to violate the rights of others — to steal, deliberately damage another's good name or property, cheat, not to pay one's debts. Respecting God's gift of life, the Christian cannot be anti-life and must avoid sins of murder, abortion, euthanasia, genocide, indiscriminate acts of war. He must not use immoral methods of family limitation. Sins of lying, detraction and calumny are forbidden, as are anger, hatred, racism and discrimination. In the area of sexuality, the Christian is to be modest in behavior and dress. In a sex-saturated society, the follower of Christ must be different. For the Christian there can be no premarital sex, fornication, adultery, or other acts of impurity or scandal to others. He must remain chaste, repelling lustful desires and temptations, self-abuse, pornography and indecent entertainment of every description" *(Basic Teaching, 19).*

Study the above paragraph carefully. It leaves no doubt that the official voice of Jesus in

His Church is specific regarding morality. Notice that the Church tells us that we *must be different* from the world. St. Maria Goretti, the 13-year-old who died to defend her virginity and purity in our own century, was different. So was Dominic Savio, the teenage saint, only 15 years old when he died. He is a model to millions of Catholic youth today in leading them in charity toward others in the concern to avoid and destroy pornography, filthy language and stories. It was this young boy's concern to lead other youth to confession for peace with God.

At the conclusion of this charter, "Charity and Morality," I am led back to the 13th chapter of First Corinthians. "Love, (that is Charity) is always patient and kind; it is never jealous; love is never boastful or conceited; it is never rude or selfish. . . . Love takes no pleasure in other people's sins but delights in the truth; it is always ready to excuse, to trust, to hope, and to endure whatever comes. . . .

"Love does not come to an end. In short, there are three things that last: faith, hope and love; and the greatest of these is love" (I Cor. 13). May I add here in the inspired words of the Apostle John, "God is love and he who abides in love abides in God and God in him." And finally, "If you keep my commandments you will remain in my love. . . ." (Jn. 15:10).

QUESTIONS FOR DISCUSSION

1. Why does the author indicate that society today is sex-saturated?
   a) Is this a lopsided or overbalanced approach to sex on the part of society?

2. Why does the author indicate that Catholic young people must be *different* from the world in their understanding of sex?

3. Explain why the author has concluded that tragedy enters the lives of those who habitually live contrary to God's laws.

4. Is sex a major or minor part of married love?
   a) Why is sex more than a pleasurable physical expression?

5. Why did God attach pleasure to sex?

6. Why is the use of sexual powers before marriage sinful but grace-filled after a valid and sacramental marriage for Christian people?

7. Answer the person who says that sex before marriage is all right because a marriage license or short ceremony doesn't change the act.

8. Who administers the Sacrament of Matrimony to the new husband and wife?

9. Give evidence from the Bible that God declares premarital sex as well as adultery by the married, seriously sinful.

10. Explain the difference between simply having a conscience and forming one's conscience *correctly*.

11. What does the Church mean when it says to Catholics that the mind and conscience of Christians must be taught and formed to recognize that there are norms which are *absolute?*

12. In an official document for the teaching of Catholic Religious Education, the Bishops of America enumerated areas of sexual abuse and sinfulness. The Holy See in turn approved of the Bishops' correct moral teaching

in this regard. Please list the areas where the Church has explained specifically correct morality in the area of sexuality.

13. Who are two modern youthful saints the Church presents for our inspiration?

14. What is meant by *Natural Law*?

    a) Why can correctly understood *Natural Law* and *Divine Law* never contradict each other?

CHAPTER III

GOD MADE SEX

God made both boys and girls. This is the same as saying, "God made sex." It was the infinite knowledge, love, beauty and power of God that deigned to make humans in His own image and likeness and to make them male and female. As human beings, men and women are equal before God with equal human rights. Yet, God made the man different from the woman. Not only are men and women different physically, there are also psychic differences. The emotional and mental differences between men and women often become the source of good humor. Men will say, "Who could ever understand a woman?" And, of course, you know what women in their turn will ask. In both cases, the question is more often a statement of the fact that God made men and women similar but different.

Sex is beautiful. Sex is sacred. The Church has always taught that. But sex does not refer only to physical differences, nor does it mean simply the marital embrace. The fact is that even the physical differences are beautiful. By their early twenties, both sexes are fully grown into young men and women. Usually the male will be taller and physically stronger. The woman's body will be more beautiful and gracious. Girls mature physically faster than boys. In general, as they reach their teen years, girls are approximately two years in advance of the boys. This will explain why a girl of 15 or 16 may consider boys the same age rather immature. Physical maturity will surely have a deep effect on emotional and mental attitudes. Give the boys time, however, and they will catch up. This helps explain why it has been traditional in many cases for a boy to be a little older than the girl in dating and marrying. Also, the man as provider usually needs more time to prepare financially to support a family.

The male figure is heavier, especially in the shoulders. The hips of the girl are larger to prepare her for her future role as a mother and the carrying of a child in the womb. Boys are more aggressive. Generally boys will be more interested in such things as sports, machines, competition. The sex glands develop quickly during the teen years. Small glands in the bodies of both boys and girls secrete hormones. The hormones of these glands cause the boy to undergo deep physical changes. His beard begins to grow. The voice becomes deeper. At times a boy will become embarrassed at some period during adolescence when his voice in unpredictable. One time his voice may be high and another time low. During class recitation a sentence begun on one pitch may end on another. All this is good, even if humorous to others and embarrassing to the boy. It is good because the male nature which God Himself created is beginning to mature in the boy.

At the same time as the beard begins to appear, hair begins to grow on the body, under the arms and about the sex organs. His male organs undergo drastic physical changes. The two testicles, suspended in the scrotum *outside* his body begin producing the life-producing cells or sperm. These sperm may be released during sleep in what is sometimes called a "wet dream." The sperm is released through the penis which is the external tube which also carries off waste water or urine. When a boy first experiences the "wet dream" he is usually frustrated and if not properly informed, he may be unnecessarily ashamed. But as we said, "God made sex" and therefore everything that God made has to be good. There is no set age when the boy will first experience the release of sperm. Usually around the age of 14 the sex glands begin to produce the sex cells or sperm. The nocturnal emission, as it is more properly called, is a natural happening.

The boy who awakens during the night to discover that an emission has just happened or is in the process of happening should not become alarmed. God is the author of nature so what is *naturally* taking place cannot be wrong. At about the same age as the boy has these experiences, he also experiences from time to time that the penis becomes temporarily erect and larger. Again, all this is an indication that he is growing in physical maturity and God is preparing him for his future role as a father and husband. In a later chapter we shall discuss the morality of some who would deliberately abuse such powers, either alone or with others, but for the present chapter, it is important to remember that no natural bodily function is evil and all that God has created is good.

In the case of the girl, the female sex hormones are secreted by glands *inside* her body. These also cause the girl to grow hair under her arms and about the sex organs. The breasts or milk glands begin to enlarge and fill out, contributing to the beauty of the female body as well as to the practical function God has in mind for the future mother. The girl is becoming a young lady and she is changing not only in appearance but also in interests. The sexual system of the girl has a process that influences her whole life, including her mental attitudes and emotions.

Just as the boy who at the age of 14 or 15 begins to experience emissions occasionally during sleep, so the girl has a similar but very different experience. A major sign of the sexual development of the girl's body will be her monthly flow of blood. At first this wonderful operation of nature will startle or deeply frighten the girl who is not properly informed that this too is part of God's plan in creation. There is no hard and fast physical rule for the girl's menstrual flow but doctors say it happens, on the average, once a month. This experience means a girl is growing up and her body is being prepared for motherhood.

The female ovum or egg is no bigger than a pin-point and is formed by the two internal ovaries. Both the ovum of the female and the sperm of the male contain the substance or chromosomes which go into the make-up of the child. Within the body of the adolescent girl, there is normally produced just one life seed each month. The adolescent girl is normally in no circumstance to become a mother and marriage may be some years off. Therefore the ovum or egg is carried off with the monthly flow of blood. When the young lady is married and in a circumstance where motherhood is possible and proper, then, if as a result of the marriage act called intercourse the male sperm of her husband unites with the egg (ovum), the monthly flow of blood will discontinue for the next nine months at least. During these months the woman's body will need all its strength and nourishment to provide for the new human life, so precious to God and man, developing within her womb and endowed with an immortal soul by a separate act of God's creation.

Modern technology has developed practical measures for assisting the young lady to use ways to absorb the fluids in a sanitary manner that will contribute to mental well-being and physical hygiene, in the case of the young lady who experiences the monthly period or menstruation, or the married woman who does not conceive.

Whereas the average girl developing into a woman usually produces but a single seed per month, the case with the boy is strikingly different. The male seeds or sperm in the boy are developed in great quantities. Each male sperm, of course, is in itself too small to be seen. A single emission may contain many thousands of sperm contained in a fluid called semen. While we do not wish to indicate that sex is impure in itself, this can and often does mean that the challenge for purity, so as not to abuse the sexual powers, can be even greater for the boy than it is for the girl.

The average boy will be more tempted toward the use of sex before marriage. The girl will normally be more calm, untroubled and she may not realize the problems boys can have in this area.

The purpose of this book is in not to give a detailed explanation of every aspect of sexual activity in marriage. There are no two couples, even in marriage, exactly alike. In a book dedicated to charity, morality, sex and young people, however, it is essential that at least the fundamental aspects of biological differences be indicated and understood. When both boys and girls, young unmarried men and women, have at least the fundamental understanding of their physical, mental and emotional differences, they are better able to help one another grow as human persons and stay close to God.

It is sometimes said that God has made girls stronger spiritually and boys stronger physically and they need to help each other. From a natural point of view, there is some truth to that. While the temptations and problems of boys may be greater, we must remember that God always gives sufficient grace and does not promise greater graces to girls than to boys. God has made both sexes in His own image and likeness and both reflect the infinite goodness and beauty of God in their special way. God has promised everyone, both girls and boys, men and women, that He will permit no one to be tempted beyond his strength.

Because the boy's organs are external, and the seeds within his organs are constant and generous, he can be more easily, quickly and even violently aroused to sexual excitement. This is something girls must remember well in their dress, actions and behavior. The girl who dresses to expose rather than to cover the private parts of the body may well be an occasion of serious temptation to the boy or young man, even leading him to serious sin. The girl who seeks affection by throwing herself into the arms of the boy or enticing him by words and manners, may have little consideration for the difficult challenge it is for the boy to control his sexual powers.

It is natural for a girl to want to feel that she is attractive and that she is loved. She desires expressions of affection. There is the possibility that she is concerned only with her popularity. She may deliberately throw temptation in the way of boys, not realizing she is appealing not to the deep, inner qualities of manliness and goodness of boys, but enticing their lower natures which is one with animals. Now, again, we must state here, that sexual powers in human beings is not entirely animal. Removed and separated from the total human person, from the higher qualities of intellect and the spiritual qualities of soul, the laws of God which express the will or love of God, sex could be reduced only to the animal level. The girl who overplays, who gives in to the *play boy* approach, may appear to be popular. But, in fact, she may be the object of ill humor and scorn for boys. She will, in fact, be the occasion of moral disgust to the boy or young man who is truly Christian in attitude and moral principles.

By the same token, we must admit that there will be some boys who make no effort at developing moral self control. Some boys think that sex is just for fun. There are *no* double standards of morality in the area of sex. There is not one standard

for boys and another for girls. Just as the standard
of sexual morality *before God* is the same between
peoples of all religions, nationalities and cultures,
so what is wrong for girls is equally wrong for boys.

When we have at least a basic understanding
of the physical differences between boys and girls,
we are in a better position to understand their
emotional and mental differences. Truth is truth
for both men and women. However, the mind of
the woman may well notice shades unnoticed by
the man. The man may well express objective fea-
tures glided over by the mind of the woman. The
man may arrive at a conclusion much more slowly
and logically, having thought out all the possibli-
ties, having exercised his mind step by step
through reasoning processes. He may be surprised
to learn that his conclusion will often coincide
with that which the woman expressed suddenly,
almost at once, by instinct. The man may admit
the woman was often correct in her impulsive conclusion, guided by emotions it would seem, or at
least womanly intuition, yet, the man will say,
"she never mentions — the times she was wrong."
The woman may well respond, "he remembers the
time I was wrong, but forgets about the times I
was correct."

The couple who go out for an evening, attend-
ing the same social function, may have some interesting conclusions that at first seem totally different, but may not be different in truth at all.
One mind may have noticed certain aspects of
truths while the other mind was observing other
aspects of the same truths. It is said that the mind
of the woman is attuned more to people and the
mind of man more to things. The mind of woman

will consider emotions and the mind of man objective facts, often with little consideration for emotional qualities.

All this is a hint at why women make better mothers and men make better fathers. The mother considers the total make-up of the child. The mother senses the emotional responses and needs of the child. The father will often consider purely objective situations and not advert to a deeper human feeling a child may be experiencing. The mother, however, has sensed that deeper inner frustration of the child instinctively. I like to think of the mother representing the *mercy* of God while the father represents the *justice* of God over children and the two, husband and wife, mother and father, working together in harmony blend to create a beautiful home atmosphere of love and righteousness.

When God made two sexes, as Scripture will attest, He made them *good.* He made them to help each other. He made them to complement each other and together they image God Himself in some measure. When the love of husband and wife is holy and true, the fruit of their love is often found in children whom God again has made in His own image and likeness. In the plan of God new human life is always to be the fruit of human love that is holy and good. In the sexual embrace of intercourse, the man places the male organ in a state of erection within the woman's body. Then both husband and wife unite in muscular responses and movements that are highly pleasurable. All this is so holy when done in accord with *God's will and mind,* that it glorifies the Creator and is a source of grace for the couple. What must be remembered is that this is *not just a union of bodies.* In true Christian sacramental marriage, it is a *union of persons,* a blending of human personalities who love each other deeply in every aspect of life. It is truly a *spiritual* union. Unless the sexual union is *accompanied* and *preceded* by a spiritual union of persons, the physical union could finally divide more than unite. It could destroy unity rather than build the heads of the family in unifying love. Sex without charity is disastrous.

It is precisely here that young people are liable to miss the most fundamental and crucial aspects regarding sex. They may consider only the biological aspects. They may consider only the pleasurable aspects from the sensual point of view. And again, we can understand this for there is so much in modern media of communications which gives this false or at least incomplete picture. This is one reason why I chose to write this book. Many a sex education course has dealt too much with detailed biological information and not sufficiently with morality and with the spiritual aspects of which the physical is merely the human expression. Sex isolated from morality, sex isolated from Christian charity, could destroy the human race. We see this in the case of abortion. We see it reflected in the contraceptive mentality. We see it in the growing numbers of families destroyed through divorce.

Unhappily, some people have been drawn to marriage only by sexual attraction. If marriage becomes only an occasion for sexual activities, without that deeper sanctifying inter-personal relationship of inner love between husband and wife, then the marriage will, at best, lack the full happiness intended by God for married people. This is not to indicate that the sexual attraction is bad. Again we must say, in itself it is good. But if attraction of man for woman and woman for man remains only on the physical sexual level, and does not penetrate to that inner reality that makes each one a unique person, capable of being known and loved for himself in Christ, then there is danger of unhappiness in time and in eternity.

Unless God is calling you to that vocation of the single life in the world, or as a priest or religious, in which case you sacrifice your sexual powers for a greater good and for the love of God, it is the plan of God for the average person to work out his salvation in company with a person of the complementary sex. "It is not good for man to be alone" (Gn. 2:18). You see then how important it is for Catholic boys and girls to develop a healthy, Christian attitude toward sex according to the mind of God. *Even working out our salvation involves sex.* If sex is a part of marriage and most people are called by God to the holy vocation of Matrimony, it follows that the proper use of sex is wrapped up in attaining salvation along with all other aspects of Christian morality and charity.

The Church does not require its priests and religious to remain single and to live celibate lives because the Church considers sex evil. *Far from it.* The Church considers sex sacred. The person called to the priesthood and religious life is asked to give up what is good for a higher good. It is for the kingdom of God that some young people give up their rights to marriage and the use of sex within marriage.

The Catholic Church considers celibacy so

important to the priesthood that it has demanded it as a pre-requisite for ordination. St. Paul admits in the Bible that "not all are capable of this, but only those to whom it is given" (Mt. 19:11; 1 Cor. 7:7). Man's ultimate and lasting fulfillment, the Church has declared, can be found only in God and in heaven. The Church teaches that priestly celibacy is a living reminder and a proclamation that our ultimate fulfillment will be in heaven where the Bible teaches that there shall be no marrying or giving in marriage. Those who are celibate *for the sake of Christ* are a witness to our future life in heaven. I personally loved the answer that was given to those who argued against celibacy as a requisite for the Catholic priesthood when they declared that an unmarried man is only half a man. The answer came back clearly, "then Jesus Christ was only half a man." Now no sincere Christian could hold that the God-man, Jesus Christ, our Lord and Savior was anything less than perfect. Yet, He did not choose marriage for Himself. He did sanctify marriage, however, at the wedding feast of Cana. His Blessed Mother and the Apostles were also there.

The priest and religious do not give up that special love that man and wife have for each other to create a *negative* emptiness and suppression. The purpose is rather to create an emptiness so that the void can be filled with love of God and of men for the sake of God. In this way there is to be no competition for deepest affections and loyalties. What the priest and religious do in making their vows is a very *positive* spiritual act. These people are in a sense *married to Christ*. The Church has long spoken of the spiritual nuptials with Christ such souls enjoy. There is a serious need today for generous young people to consider seriously such sacrificial love in the name of Christ Jesus by giving their lives as priests or religious. They become also a testimony to married people that sexual love can be kept within reasonable and moral bounds. They are a source of encouragement to young unmarried people that a life of purity is possible.

Every priest should experience spiritual fatherhood. The good religious Sister will experience spiritual motherhood in the children she teaches, in bodies and souls she nurses. Speaking from experience as a priest whom people call "Father," I do not think I could ever have been satisfied with a few children that a physical father must content himself with, even when that family numbers eight or ten children. My desire to be a spiritual Father *in Christ* has found need to extend itself to hundreds, even thousands of souls, not only in my parish family but even in my apostolate of the pen.

Priests and religious do not give up their sexuality. The manly and womanly qualities, the differences of mind, emotional responses, remain. Only in a life totally dedicated and consecrated to the kingdom of God are these powers supernaturalized. The priest uses his manly qualities for communicating the Word of God in His divine love to all men; so too the religious Brother. The Sister consecrates her womanly qualities as a spiritual mother to countless souls.

QUESTIONS FOR DISCUSSION
1. Why is sex sacred?

2. Who matures at an earlier age, a boy or a girl?

3. Who experiences stronger sexual drives, a boy or a girl?

4. Does God necessarily give greater grace to girls than to boys?

5. Do you think the average boy really wants a girl to lower her standards in the area of sexual morality?

6. Are there differences in the emotional and mental qualities of boys and girls?

    a) Give some examples of how a young man or woman may view things differently.

7. Explain the following statement: "The mystery of sex has long interested mankind because essentially, in the plan of God, it involves the spiritual union of husband and wife in their total persons."

    a) Explain: "Sex without charity is disastrous."

8. Explain: "One who is drawn to marriage only by sex attraction for the sake of selfish pleasure will be in danger of unhappiness in time and in eternity."

9. Explain how the Church requires celibacy of its priests and religious for a higher good.

    a) How does a priest experience fatherhood in the fulfillment of his God-given vocation?

    b) How does the woman religious experience motherhood?

CHAPTER IV

THE CATHOLIC CONSCIENCE AND THE TEACHING CHURCH

As well instructed and informed Catholic boys and girls know, they have been gifted with the fullness of the true Christian faith. Still we must not look down our noses at our fellow Christians who are not Catholic. God has been good to them too. They have much that is good and true in their faith. But the Church clearly teaches that we must not compromise our own faith and morals. Jesus Christ founded one Church. He founded, as history attests, the Catholic Church almost 2000 years ago. Jesus promised that the Church He established upon earth would never be destroyed. You Catholic boys and girls have been given the *fullness* of that faith.

You have all the seven sacraments, not just part of them. You receive the living and substantial Body, Blood, Soul and Divinity of our Lord and Savior Jesus Christ every time you receive Him in Holy Communion. You have the sacrament of Penance, more frequently called "confession," whereby you can know that the very Person of Jesus Christ acts to forgive you your sins, and restore or increase sanctifying grace in your soul. At every Holy Mass in which you participate, you are actually taking part in the perpetuation of the Sacrifice of the Cross, the infinite act of worship of the Christian community. Through no good merits of your own, (and I can say the same for myself and every other Catholic), but only through the goodness of Almighty God, you have been given the gift of the fullness of true faith. Of those to whom God has given more, He will expect more. In a world grown cold in charity and permissive in sexuality then, you Catholic boys and girls (tomorrow's parents and tomorrow's priests and religious) will have to be the instruments of Christ in renewing all things in Him Who is the Way, the Truth and the Life.

How sad it is to pick up the papers and read the results of some recent survey and discover, in some cases, that there was little difference registered between the moral attitudes of Catholic young people and the attitudes of others not gifted with the fullness of faith. Frankly, I am often mistrustful of surveys. It has been my own experience that the Catholic boys and girls of my acquaintance have almost overwhelmingly and without exception accepted the authentic teachings of the holy Catholic and Apostolic Church. I have found it to be a rare Catholic young person who, once honestly and completely informed on Catholic faith and morals, has ever rejected them outright. However, I've discovered that *some* Catholic young people may be confused about the authentic teaching of the Church on faith and morals. When that is the case, usually it is not their own fault, but due to the carelessness or scandal of parents or someone who should have presented the true teachings of Jesus but chose rather to pass personal frustrations and anxiety onto youth. *But young people want to know the truth.* When it is a challenge, when it demands taking up the Cross of Jesus, most young people will do so.

Pope Paul VI will go down in history as the Pope who was *pro-life.* In the face of difficulties, opposing pressures from all over the world, on July 25, 1968 this Pope issued an encyclical letter titled: *Humanae Vitae* (Of Human Life). There were those, even within the Church, including some in influential places, urging the Pope to change the Church's traditional moral teachings which forbid artificial birth control in any form. The Pope said this:

"In the task of transmitting life, therefore, they (husband and wife) are not free to proceed completely at will, as if they could determine in a wholly autonomous way the honest path to follow; but they must conform their activity to the creative intention of God, expressed in the very nature of marriage and of its acts, and manifested by the constant teaching of the Church.

"These acts, by which husband and wife are united in chaste intimacy, and by means of which human life is transmitted, are, as the council recalled, 'noble and worthy,' and they do not cease to be lawful if, for causes independent of the will of husband and wife, they are foreseen to be infecund, since they always remain ordained towards expressing and consolidating their union.

In fact, as experience bears witness, not every conjugal act is followed by a new life. God has wisely disposed natural laws and rhythms of fecundity which, of themselves, cause a separation in the succession of births. Nonetheless the Church, calling men back to the observance of the norms of the natural law, as interpreted by their constant doctrine, teaches that each and every marriage act must remain open to the transmission of life."

The Pope was not saying something new. Yet, when he made that statement, some Catholics publicly protested the official teaching of the Church. In fact, they did not wait to read the entire encyclical letter of the Pope, "Of Human Life." They immediately "went public" and issued statements in disagreement with the Pope who is the Vicar of Jesus Christ upon earth and to whom we must listen and obey before all else. Why must we listen to him? Because the Pope, before everyone else in the Church, speaks for Jesus Christ. The Pope, in *Of Human Life,* was saying that love-giving and life-giving cannot be separated.

Less than five years after Catholic spokesmen took to the public media attacking their own Church, the Supreme Court of the United States on that Black Monday in January of 1973 legalized abortive murders. It was a result of the breakdown in sexual morality. The contraceptive mentality had led to the legalization of hundreds of thousands of abortions, which are in reality the murder of unborn babies. Those who rejected the Pope in his restating the constant faith and morals of the Church regarding "responsible parenthood" share much of the guilt for scattering the strength of the authentic Catholic voice for Christ Jesus and for the unborn. Confusing the nation, confusing many Catholic peoples in their consciences about artificial birth control, the path was laid for a contraceptive mentality. This led to an abortive mentality. An abortion is not just the removal of some tissue, as some are led to believe. It is the destruction of *human life.* Scientists verify that.

Those who first took to the media protesting *Of Human Life* did so even before they had time to read the actual encyclical letter of the Pope. The night before it was made public, they were already making phone calls across the nation, eliciting support to protest the official voice of the Church. The total message of that momentous encyclical was thus lost to many. At no time had the Pope ever indicated that the Church would change its teachings. The Pope, speaking for Christ, did what he had to do. He was convinced that *Of Human Life* represented divine law, the will of God, which could not be changed. The Church may change only man-made laws. She may not change what is divine law, which comes directly from God.

Those who would confuse the faithful and say that we may ignore the Pope even when he issues an Encyclical Letter on matters of faith or morals have often been heard to say this. "We are the Church, too." Now it is true that all baptized people are in some way members of the Church of Christ. But there is only one *visible* head of the Church and that is the Pope. (Jesus is the invisible head.) It is absolutely wrong to say that in forming a correct conscience we need merely to consider the voice of the Church, officially stated by the Pope, as just another opinion worthy of consideration. Pope Pius XII in *Humani Generis* of 1950 clearly stated that when the Pope issues a statement in an encyclical letter matters are concluded and we have a sure guidance.

The Pope teaches the true faith, not because people consent to or agree with what he teaches. The Pope rather teaches true faith because the Holy Spirit, acting chiefly through the Pope, keeps the Catholic Church in the truth. The Pope may speak one time on the Holy Eucharist. Another time the Pope may speak on Mary, or how to live a life of purity. We must always accept what the Pope says before everyone else. Then we are listening to Jesus. Even in his day to day ordinary teachings, we must listen to the Pope for he often applies the constant true faith to present situations.

Surely the Pope was aware that a contraceptive mentality would lead to a total breakdown in sexual morality. He foresaw the consequences of abortion. He stated in *Of Human Life:* "In conformity with these landmarks in the human and Christian vision of marriage, we must once again declare that the direct interruption of the generative process already begun, and, above all, *directly willed and procured abortion,* even if for therapeutic reasons, are to be absolutely excluded as licit means of regulating birth." He continued, "Equally to be excluded, as the teaching authority of the Church has frequently declared, is direct sterilization, whether perpetual or temporary, whether of the man or of the woman. Similarly

excluded is every action which, either in antici-
pation of the conjugal act, or in its accomplish-
ment, or in the development of its natural consequences, proposes, whether as an end or as a
means, to render procreation impossible."

In an attempt to further confuse Catholic
people, after the Pope restated the constant
teachings of the Church regarding human sexuality, rumors were circulated that national confer-
ences of Catholic Bishops themselves rejected the
Pope's encyclical letter *Of Human Life.* Such
groups of bishops were often misrepresented. As a
matter of fact, even had the rumors proved true, it
would not have justified rejecting the official
voice of the Church which speaks for Jesus in the
Vicar of Christ, the Pope. As a matter of fact, it
would not have been the first time some bishops
were led astray. A study of the heresy of Arianism,
condemned by the Council of Nicaea in 325, will
testify to that.

Although the secular press misrepresented
our American Bishops in their Pastoral supporting the Pope's Encyclical Letter, our U.S. Bishops
in fact did speak as follows:

"The sacredness of Christian marriage makes
it a special concern of the teaching mission of the
Church. Its dignity must be carefully safeguarded
and its responsibilities fulfilled. The recent encyclical letter of Pope Paul VI reflects this concern.

"The Holy Father, speaking as the supreme
teacher of the Church, has reaffirmed the principles to be followed in forming the Christian consciences of married persons in carrying out their
responsibilities.

"Recognizing his unique role in the Universal

Church, we, the bishops of the Church in the United States, unite with him in calling upon our priests and people to receive with sincerity what he has taught, to study it carefully, and to form their consciences in its light.

"We are aware of the difficulties that this teaching lays upon so many of our conscientious married people. But we must face the reality that struggling to live out the will of God will often entail sacrifice.

"In confident trust in the firmness of their faith, in their loyalty to the Holy Father and to his office, and their reliance on Divine help, we ask of them a true Christian response to this teaching."

The Mexican bishops and the Canadian bishops were also misrepresented. It is easy to take statements out of context and to report a slanted meaning. When the Mexican bishops realized how their statements were interpreted or misrepresented, they too had to make clarifications. The Canadian bishops by the end of 1973 still found it necessary to issue their "Statement on the Formation of Conscience."

This is what the Canadian bishops said in their statement on conscience. "To follow one's conscience and to remain a Catholic, one must take into account first and foremost the teaching of the magisterium (the Church's teaching authority). For a Catholic to follow one's conscience is not, then, simply to act as his unguided reason dictates," they said. The bishops explained conscience as "that ultimate judgment that every man is called to make as to whether this or that action is acceptable to him without violating the principles which he is prepared to admit as governing his life. If he goes against those principles, he is said to be acting against his conscience."

Conscience, these bishops said, is "not simply some still, small voice which is evoked by some mysterious mechanism within us when we are faced with a practical decision as to whether a given course of action is acceptable or not. When doubt arises due to a conflict of my views and those of the magisterium, the presumption of truth lies on the part of the magisterium," the bishops said.

The Canadian bishops also stated, as did the U.S. bishops in their November 21, 1973 *Marian Pastoral,* that there must be a religious submission of mind and will to the authentic teaching authority of the Pope — even when he is not speaking *ex cathedra,* that is when he exercises the authority of his office in defining a doctrine concerning faith and morals to be held by the whole Church. In other words, the Church presents the authentic faith in its day to day teaching, not only when it solemnly defines a matter of faith or morals.

The bishops of Canada, in agreement with our own bishops of the United States, said that such papal teaching, "must be carefully distinguished from the teaching of individual theologians or individual priests, however intelligent or persuasive." Contributing factors to confusion in the minds of many, these bishops said, are: the notion that if something is legal it must be moral; widespread propaganda concerning sexual permissiveness; individualistic ethics; economic inequalities; and the depersonalization of society and the exploitation of man.

I have included in this chapter much that will concern your consciences if and when you young people are called to the holy state of matrimony. It is often typical of teenagers to be concerned only with the *now*. Experience teaches, however, that during these, your crucial developmental years, it is essential that you be properly formed in authentic Christian and Catholic consciences to guide you in your adult years. You must be prepared to stand by Christ. The world is forever attempting to take the cross out of Christianity. When Jesus hung dying on the cross, men called up to Him, "If you are God's Son, come down from the cross! . . . Let him come down from the cross now, and we will believe in him" (Mt. 27:42-43). That is what men today have cried to the Pope, the Vicar of Jesus Christ, "let him take the cross out of Christianity, let him not require any sacrifice, then we will believe." Nonsense. Some men refused to believe in Jesus even after He rose from the dead.

The proponents of artificial contraception have promised many social advantages. They have promised less divorce, less juvenile delinquency, less poverty and more family stability. These advocates have been wrong on all counts. There is rising divorce, more juvenile delinquency, increasing poverty and the breakdown of family life to such a serious degree that some have even feared that the family institution would eventually fade away. Man cannot improve on God's commandments. They are established by God and built into human nature. Their obedience is essential for man's happiness in time and in eternity.

It is true that the thrust of the Pope's teaching in *Of Human Life* which was against contraception was based on natural law. But it was also based on natural law which was *illumined and enriched by Divine Revelation.* It was based on the Word of God, not simply on man's reasoning power. It was Cardinal Shehan who rightly stated: "The case for prohibition of contraception is, from a Scriptural point of view, as strong or even stronger" than in the past, but it is implicit. The "light shed by Scripture on contraception as being against the ethos of the content of the Old and New Testaments is significant. . . ."

A book came out as a best seller in 1973 that should interest conscientious Catholic young people and others: *Handbook on Population.* The author is Dr. Robert L. Sassone who has ten years of college credits, including degrees in Physics from the University of Michigan, and Law from Loyola University, Los Angeles. He has traveled around the world, studying all major nations of high population density. In his book he offers a $1,000 reward to anyone "for proving the validity of any reason why population growth must be limited within the next century." He has made his offer repeatedly in debates with advocates of population stagnation. *There have been no serious claims for the reward.* The general response made by Zero Population Growth advocates is that while they themselves are not skilled and do not know the facts, they believe that someone else does, and that there is a population problem. Dr. Sassone has been honored in "Who's Who in the West" because of his work in population and for arguing the rights of unborn human beings.

The observation of Dr. Sassone that everyone keeps repeating the population panic scare is typical. No one offers anything concrete. The contraception and consequent abortive mentality have been dominating. He says, "the more panic is sold, the more it seems to sell." Today's young people had better do some serious study on the matter both from the point of view of their faith and from solid research into the reliability of the overpopulation panickers. We who live in the Dakotas, or anyone who travels by car across this great country of ours, can become aware of the statistics usually *not* quoted. All farms, roads, cities and buildings combined take up about three percent of the earth's surface. Land area is about 30 percent of the earth's surface. All buildings take up less than 0.01 percent of the earth's surface. This is contrary to the pictures which show people standing 10 high on each other's heads.

"The end does not justify the means." That is a moral principle today's young people should become well acquainted with and have sink deeply into their moral consciences. One cannot use an evil means to accomplish what he *thinks* (and often thinks wrongly) is a good end. The next step from abortion is euthanasia. There have already been legal attempts in that direction. The brave new world in which today's young people will find themselves tomorrow, if the population alarmists have their way, will be one in which women are grudgingly forgiven the first time they give birth, but are spayed like a female dog for their second offense. It is a world in which the weak have only those rights the strong care to give them. It is a world in which a woman who gives birth is de-

spised and a woman who aborts her unborn baby is given a medal. It is a world in which there are far too many old people and far too few young, working people, so that it becomes necessary to destroy those old people whose lives are "meaningless." It is a world in which all old people's lives are meaningless. It is a world in which the spirit of Hitler reigns supreme over all human dignity. The breakdown in sexual morality and disregarding Christ's voice in the Teaching Church will surely lead to this world. Where will you be?

QUESTIONS FOR DISCUSSION

1. Explain: In respecting goodness and sincerity in the faith of other Christians, Catholics should not compromise their own faith.
2. Explain: Some Catholic boys and girls who appear to have rejected the Catholic faith have never really understood it correctly.
3. Why will Pope Paul VI, according to the author, go down in history as the Pope who was *pro-life*?
4. In stating the official position of the Catholic Church in his encyclical which forbade artificial birth control, was Pope Paul stating something new or was he declaring what had long been the constant teaching of the Church?
5. Why does the author of this book (along with many others) hold that those, even within the Church, who publicly protested the Pope in his *pro-life* encyclical, laid much ground work for the Black Monday of January 22, 1973, which saw the U.S. Supreme Court legalizing abortive murders?

6. Explain: The Pope saw that a contraceptive mentality would lead to a total breakdown in sexual morality and was already leading to it.

7. How have the American bishops as a whole responded to the Pope's teaching on the transmission of human life?

8. Explain this statement of our bishops: "When doubt arises due to a conflict of my views and those of the magisterium, the presumption of truth lies on the part of the magisterium."

9. Explain the statement of the bishops of Canada which indicated that just because something is legal it is not necessarily moral.

   a) Whose teaching authority did these bishops consider of most importance?

10. Explain: "The world is forever attempting to take the Cross out of Christianity."

11. What is meant by Natural Law?

12. Explain: *Of Human Life* is based not simply on the Natural Law, but on law as illumined and enriched by Divine Revelation.

13. What is meant by: *the end does not justify the means.*

   a) Give an example where the end would not justify the means.

CHAPTER V

THE RESTLESS YEARS — YEARS OF TRANSITION

But what about *Now*? What is sinful *now*? What is morally permissible *now*? The young man and woman want to know. They have a right to know. The simplicity of childhood is gone forever. In pre-adolescent years, the sexual appetite was dormant. The latency period was intended by God as a time of innocence and complete trust in parents. In those days your life was relatively untroubled and free of worries. There is a time during pre-adolescence when boys and girls almost seem like natural enemies. To little boys, girls seem weak and silly. To the girls, the boys seem noisy, rude and rough.

Confession was no big problem for boys and girls in the lower grades. Venial sins of disobedience of parents, fighting with friends, unkindness, such seemed the most to worry about. And, oh yes, you did not pray as well as you could have. You didn't even mind if Father knew who you were when you went to confession. You might

THE RESTLESS YEARS 67

even walk up to Father and say, "Are you going to hear my confession now, Father?" And as for having anything to confess against purity, why you didn't know what a temptation against sex meant, unless it was pulling some little girl's hair or getting angry at some little rude boy. Impurity may have meant not washing your face and hands or not keeping your clothes clean. But then something happened. Boys were no longer just noisy creatures and girls were no longer sissies. They actually became attractive to each other.

You can tell when a boy is becoming conscious of the other sex. He begins to take a sharper notice of his appearance. The young lady becomes more conscious of how to act graciously, ladylike in dress and action. Boys and girls, as they arrive at the teen years, become not only interested in one another but also curious about each other. Both boys and girls are aware of physical changes taking place in their bodies. Oftentimes their minds are filled with thoughts that do not please even themselves and they wish they once again knew some of the peace and quiet of former years when life was more calm and less troubled. The adolescent boy and girl become uncertain of themselves. They are attracted to the opposite sex, yet they do not quite know what to make of their new experiences and desires. Is it good or is it evil?

The problems normal to young people are not helped by the pornography so abundant today. It gives an exaggerated notion of sex and is entirely devoid of God and His plan. In the attempt to make sex attractive, filthy literature and pictures instead make it ugly and desecrate the beauty of

what God has created. There is always the wise
guy or gal who is "in the know" and desires to in-
form the other teenagers, but is in reality the least
qualified to do so. Their attitude is wrong and
their information is usually faulty.

If the teenaged boy is not careful, and gets a
warped notion of sex, he may come to regard girls
only as "things" and not as persons. This attitude
could carry into physical adulthood. The girl, if
she is not careful, coming to a realization of the
aggressiveness of boys, may misinterpret them
and conclude that every boy is primarily only
after sexual pleasure. She may fail to realize how
she can bring out the goodness in boys by being
more of a lady and demanding the respect due ladies. The girl who does not have a wholesome and
true Christian attitude on sex, may use only her
sexual attractiveness without offering an alert
and pleasant personality. She may never be accepted and liked for the kind of person she is.

At times one sees it on the movie screen, in
magazines or on television. The girl with little talent may have little more than a sexy body to offer
and she throws herself around in the most unbe-
coming way, a way that is disgusting to any lady
or gentleman of healthy, Christian conscience and
dignity. The upright Christian boy and girl know
that development will mean more than development of sexual powers. There should be a development of the total person: the intellect, the will,
social graces, self control, a generous spirit, the
willingness to help others be good and improve
themselves.

While it is normal for boys to want to have
strong bodies and develop their physical prowess,

yet, manhood is not solely determined by who is the strongest or the greatest athlete. Some of the greatest men the world has known have been physically handicapped. They were real men because they had deep manly, courageous and understanding qualities. The boy who realizes girls are attracted to him only because of his brawn should not be flattered. It takes more of a man to develop talents of grace, poise, to be gentlemanly, understanding, forgiving, kind and generous. There are many talents to be developed. God does not give everyone the same talents and muscle is never a chief talent.

The couple who marry for physical qualities alone risk having their marriage end in disaster. It is still true that beauty is only skin deep. This saying refers, of course, to *physical* beauty. Many young men and women who may not appear attractive or beautiful are most popular. Why? Because they have developed outgoing personalities that are generous, self-sacrificing, concerned about others, cheerful.

I recall the story a good mother once told me about her attractive teenage daughter, who in her senior year in high school had been talking about that very special boy in school the girls were excited about. Finally a dream came true. That very special boy, that attractive Romeo, asked the attractive senior girl for a date. The week before, the mother related to me, there was curiosity at home. The mother could hardly wait to meet the boy that had proved such a challenge to the girls. He must really be a handsome young man, she thought, something to behold. The hour arrived. The doorbell rang. The teenage girl dashed for the door to bring the boy to meet her mother. The boy was not too tall, not too well-built, had pimples and wore glasses. The mother concluded that the boy was attractive to the girls because of his personality, his inner spirit, his soul. The beauty of his person was unknown and unnoticed to the casual observer.

Then there was the very handsome man I remember. God had endowed him with a well-built body, and a face easy to look at. This young man could have almost any girl he wanted. Surely he would come some day with a strikingly beautiful bride. And oh! What a handsome and beautiful couple they would make. Yet the young lady he picked for his bride was thought by most to be anything but beautiful. Not only was she common in appearance, she had less than average good looks. But this was the girl for him. And she was beautiful, inside. He saw the beauty beneath the skin, her person. And they were a beautiful couple and had a successful marriage.

Then there is the story of the man gifted with an intellect of genius. His intellectual powers, well developed, were widely recognized. He met a beautiful lady, not known for any particular intellectual abilities. She was attracted to him and so she presented to him what she thought would be a challenging thought to consider marriage. "Just think what a wonderful family would be ours. The children would have my looks and your brains." To this the man, highly intellectual but not too handsome answered, "But think, my dear, they could have your brains and my looks."

In the plan of God, curiosity of boys and girls for each other begins to manifest itself during adolescence. This curiosity is not restricted to just one boy or girl but to the opposite sex in general. There is something mysterious about sex. God intended it to be so. But underneath the biological differences is the mystery of the inner person created in God's image. God Himself is that infinite Mystery of faith. If human persons are created in God's own image and likeness, the art of getting to know the other person intimately is the work of a lifetime. There is something mysterious in human nature. Each person is unique. This is what Pope Paul VI said of conjugal love in his famous encyclical *Of Human Life:*

> *This love is first of all fully human, that is to say, of the senses and of the spirit at the same time. It is not, then, a simple transport of instinct and sentiment, but also, and principally, an act of the free will, intended to endure and to grow by means of the joys and sorrows of daily life, in such a way that husband and wife become one only heart and one only soul, and together attain their human perfection.*

As the boy and girl advance in age into young adulthood, their interest in the opposite sex will finally culminate in one particular man, in one particular woman. In fact, that is the meaning of the wedding ring. The wedding ring is an external symbol that this husband, that this wife, have henceforth restricted all conjugal affection solely to the married partner. The wedding ring is an outward sign that the person wearing it is committed *for life* to one person in Christ.

So serious is this law of God (not simply a law of the Church), that marriage lasts until death, that "what God has joined together, let no man put asunder," that should either the husband or wife break their marriage vows and fall into the mortal sin of adultery after marriage, the innocent party would be entitled to request of the Bishop a *separation* until death. Mind you, we did *not* say that the Church would declare them divorced or their marriage dissolved, for marriage lasts until death. When there has been a valid, consummated and sacramental marriage, there is no such thing as a divorce. The State may permit divorces, but the Church cannot dissolve the true sacramental and consummated marriage. We are again reminded here that what is legal is not always morally right. In some cases the Church has declared there was *never* a true marriage to begin with, but the Church cannot "put asunder" what God has joined together. For very serious reasons, the Church may grant a *separation* but the couple *separated* with the permission of the Bishop is still married. They are *not* free to marry others.

All this indicates how careful young people must be during their dating years, to see that they find a partner who is socially compatible. They must not rush into marriages. They must not marry too young, and at whatever age they marry, they must be sufficiently knowledgeable of the other person to determine that they have a sufficient and common foundation upon which they can build for life. It is well known that an alarming number of teenage marriages end in divorce. The statistics in that regard have been climbing steadily. At this writing, nearly half of those who marry during the teen years are divorced within two years. Their lives are often ruined permanently. Often there is a child or two who will have to go through life in abnormal conditions because the parents were not ready for marriage.

Young people can often correct mistakes in other areas of life, but in the case of sexual mistakes, the covering-over, the starting-over, is not simple or even possible. Young people who think that sex is only for fun, like some game, may ruin not only their own lives, but those of their parents, and even of their innocent children. What about the pain and frustration of a child growing up without parents, or with only one parent because his real parents were never married? Life can be difficult enough normally. Think of the added difficulties in the life of such a child.

All this means that sex is sacred and powerful and must be respected and treated as such. Ultimately, sex involves human life and is the power God uses to create new human life. Boys and girls must realize that their bodies, already during the teen years, have all the faculties of reproducing new human life. They must realize also that they have absolutely no right to use those powers until they are validly married. They should not consider marriage until they are prepared psychologically, financially and spiritually to enter into a life-long commitment to one of the most serious responsibilities upon earth, the founding of a family.

Steady and exclusive courtship is designed toward marriage. Today, too many young people use it for security in their teen years when they

should be finding their security in their parents,
their home lives, in their faith. It may be comfort-
ing always to have one boy, one girl, to count on
for a date for the dance or game. But prolonged,
steady and exclusive dating all too frequently
leads to undue familiarities and to the use of the
sexual powers which spell not only serious sin but
often unwanted pregnancies and premature marriages. Remember, the sin is not in the pregnancy.
The sin is in the illicit act of intercourse, or unjustified heavy petting which led to it.

I have been dealing with teenagers for a long,
long time. I am fully aware that some of them will
argue violently that steady and exclusive dating
during the teens, when marriage is not possible or
reasonable for some years, is all right. But the
truth is, it is often an unjustified occasion of sin.
Your bodies are youthful and you are, by nature,
physically attracted to each other. It is difficult
for any young boy and girl to be alone together
frequently and for an extended period of time
without seeking undue familiarities. We are
bound in conscience to avoid unnecessary occasions of sin. An occasion of sin is any person,
place or circumstance which may easily lead us
into sin. Young people may be very good in general. Their intentions may be pure. I understand
that. But I also understand the human condition.
What frequently happens when two young and
wholesome people begin seeing each other
frequently, exclusively, and alone, familiarity and
passions grow. Finally things can get entirely out
of hand. Often a good young couple, while
warned, think their case is different. They would
never sin. And so they do not avoid the occasions.

There have been cases of parents who are foolish. Parents should know better. But some parents are flattered that their son or daughter is so popular. "She has a steady," they may brag, only later to hang their heads in shame. Teenagers whose parents are strict have every right to be proud of their parents. It is your parents' concern, therefore their love for you, that makes them appear strict at times.

As a general rule, I would state that couple dating should *not* precede the final two years in senior high school. *Group* dating, in the sense of boys and girls coming together for parties and dances, may be good before that, if properly supervised. But even in the final two years of high school, there should *not* be a steady and exclusive courtship. At the age of 16 to 18 one is hardly capable of understanding the serious responsibilities of what marriage is all about and should *not* be contemplating a life-long commitment immediately after high school graduation or shortly thereafter.

The teenaged boy or girl, the young man or woman, should become acquainted with *many* other young people. Get to know various personalities. In this way you will develop social graces and be better able to select a future husband or wife. For something so serious, that will affect your happiness in time and in eternity, and the lives of others as well, you cannot afford to make a mistake or be in a hurry in making your decision.

In the next chapter, we shall discuss the morality of dating and possible personal sins against purity which bother the consciences of some young people.

QUESTIONS FOR DISCUSSION

1. Why do developing young men and women at some point in their adolescence begin to take a more active interest in their personal appearance?

   a) Is this good?

2. Why is pornography not only a frequent and serious occasion of sin but an untrue picture of God's creation of the power of sex?

3. Discuss as true or false: The male member of the human race who is physically strong and a keen athlete best exemplifies true manhood.

4. Discuss as true or false: The young man who cooperates with the grace of God in conquering temptations is exercising his manhood more than the hero on the school's football team who scores a touchdown.

5. Discuss: A certain young man is held in high regard by good Christian girls. He is, however, not gifted physically or in appearance.

6. A young lady, by common standards, not considered beautiful, marries a young man considered not only handsome but wholesome in most every way. Others comment: "I don't see what he saw in her." Comment on their reaction.

7. How is God Himself behind the mystery of sex? (Remember the element of Person.)

8. Even though the state may declare a marriage no longer exists, why is it that the Church cannot dissolve a true sacramental and consummated marriage?

9. What possible harm could come to young people who consider sex is only for fun?

10. Steady dating here is intended to mean

frequent and exclusive dating of one person. Why have marriage counselors and Church authorities strongly discouraged steady dating among young people when marriage would not be possible or *reasonable* for some years?

11. What are the benefits of a young person having dated various boys or girls before finally beginning exclusive company keeping with one person?

12. Does a non-engaged couple really have the right to think they would do wrong by dating others?

CHAPTER VI

SEX AND THE YOUNG GIRL

In this chapter I am directing my words to young girls who are developing into young ladies. Hopefully your mothers have assisted you in understanding physical changes in your body, have taught you not only their meaning, but sanitary measures, etc. What you need to understand at this point is that there is much more to sex than the mere facts of life. You need to understand explosive emotions and how to control them.

By now it should be abundantly clear that the full use of sex outside of marriage is seriously sinful. The girl who stimulates a boy deliberately or does the same with herself alone is acting immorally. One need not be prudish. One must be reasonable. But here is a question that girls frequently wonder about. "Are the boy's feelings and thoughts about sex different from those of the girl?" It is important to realize that there is a very great difference between boys and girls, both biologically and emotionally.

It is sometimes stated this way. The young man can separate sex from love but the average young lady cannot separate love from sex. It may be true that some girls can separate love from this physical attraction but most find that their feelings of romantic love and sexual desires are closely related. For the boy, his sexual desires will come suddenly, be intense and can and often are exclusively physical with no relationship at all to the heart, to deep emotions of love and tenderness. The boy who has been sexually aroused is intent upon immediate satisfaction, a satisfaction that is physically pleasurable to release strong physical and nervous tension. Unless the girl understands this biological and psychological condition of the boy, she is very liable to mistake his urgent drives, often called "passes" as signs of tender love. The advance of a boy then is not a sure sign that he loves her.

In the earlier part of this book we explained that the popular view of love does not represent Christian love or charity. Sex is not essentially Christian love. It may be no more than a biological function totally divorced from the union of persons in their wills, in their souls. Even in the case of older boys and girls, the young Christian man and woman contemplating marriage, where there may well exist an authentic growing tenderness of the love of *hearts,* still, by the direct law of God, they may not express their love by complete sexual embrace until they are truly married in Christ. If they want their love to be Christian, to be in Christ, even before marriage, then, even though it is difficult, they must avoid occasions that put them in serious dangers because

Christ Jesus says "No." Surely a courtship of mortal sin is no preparation for the holy state of matrimony. It will at times be difficult for a young couple truly in love to remain pure. But again, God's grace is always sufficient. They must ask for God's help and avoid dangerous occasions. The girl must be fully aware of the young man's differences, physically and psychologically, and she must help him to be pure so that they both may be pure in their preparation for marriage.

Let us consider further the teenage girl who may be some years from marriage. She may feel insulted if a boy makes a pass at her. She must realize that this is part of the aggressive nature of the boy. It is not an insult to refuse a boy without unduly humiliating him as a person. We are not discussing here extreme situations where some immoral boy may act so far from Christian conduct that he is actually attempting force. The truth is this: If a boy is basically a good Christian, he is pleased and edified with the girl who knows when and how to call a halt.

What the teenage girl must remember is that she has a slower-rising sexual physical condition. At the same time she has a greater involvement in emotions associated with it than the boy does. This is really also a part of God's plan as it serves as a protection to the girl who would have to face consequences not faced by the boy. To put it bluntly, girls get pregnant and boys do not.

Counselors, psychologists, clergymen will admit that unmarried teenage girls who have lost their virginity seriously regret it afterwards. Hopefully, they also have a supernatural motive so as to repent and attain God's peace once again.

Some girls try to use sex to work out problems. The result is an increase of problems. If they were seeking security, the result is anxiety and *less* security.

As a general rule, any girl who has been seduced asked for it. Most young boys make a pass without really expecting the girl to give in. If he is any kind of a decent boy, he will lose respect for the girl who does give in. The girl who refuses and politely tells the boy she does not want such manifestations, is more likely to win the *heart* of the boy. The "fast" girl becomes known as immoral.

Why is it that the young man who may have lost his purity with the girl, will, as a general rule, want a pure girl, a virgin, to enter into marriage with him, to become the mother of his family? Is this a double standard? It would seem so. Yet, it is testimony that boys and young men respect purity and they expect girls to be strict and help them control their urgent physical drives. The girl who permits petting is asking for serious trouble. She must keep in mind that the average boy is easily aroused to the breaking point by any kind of physical contact. She cannot expect to engage in touches, heavy embraces, and not have the boy develop physical reactions that become almost impossible for him to shut off. He may not put it in words but the good young man really wants the girl to help him, even stop him.

The modest holding of hands, the gentle kiss, may be perfectly harmless. A kiss is a sacred sign of affection. The son who kisses his mother, or the girl her dad, are surely expressing signs of love that come from the heart. But God intended the strong and prolonged embrace and physical touches as a preliminary preparation for stimulation prior to sexual intercourse within marriage. If a couple are not permitted by God to have the fullest and complete expression of married love, then they must avoid those things intended to lead directly to it.

I have learned in dealing with many souls over the years that it is even dangerous to use such words as "petting" and "necking." These very terms can mean different things to different people. Let it suffice to say then, that any physical exchanges that are designed by the *unmarried* deliberately to arouse one another's physical passions are seriously sinful. It may be that a couple, while not intending to arouse the passions of the other party, will discover that this is in fact happening. The boy is becoming tense. What to do? The only thing to do is in some way *immediately* call a halt while the girl still has her state of virginity and the boy has not gone too far. To continue in any measure, even if sexual intercourse is not the final outcome, is to go too far and to be immoral. If a boy is willing to break off all relationships with a girl because she calls the danger points, such a boy is good riddance. If a boy is interested only in the body, and not the person, it is better to discover that now than to have a courtship continue that is not based on the heart, on inter-personal relationships.

What about the boy who uses this gag on the girl? "If you truly love me, you would be willing to go further." The answer would be simple. "If you truly *loved* me (with a real understanding of love), you wouldn't."

If contraceptives are forbidden to the married, they surely are doubly forbidden to the unmarried. Even from a natural point of view, there is no contraceptive yet invented that is completely safe. We have all heard of venereal disease reaching epidemic proportions. Syphilis and gonorrhea are transmitted through sexual intercourse. If not given special medical attention under the care of a doctor, such diseases can be disastrous both for the person who has contacted it and any future children. Doctors tell us that those who have contacted such diseases, first noticing the appearance of sores, should not think they are cured when the sores disappear. The disease is going deeper into the system and will later appear with physical consequences that often will be permanent and can cause death. The help of a doctor should be sought *immediately* when either a boy or girl suspect they have contacted venereal disease.

Many young girls have thought that a sexual first experience would be like the ringing of romantic bells and the trilling of bluebirds. There is often both a physical and an emotional let-down. Even for couples properly married in Christ, the compatibility in the sexual embrace may take a considerable number of months of understanding and experience. The girl who engages in pre-marital sex, in addition to offending God by serious sin, is an accomplice in the boy's serious sin. Add to this the fear of pregnancy, worry that others will discover, wondering if the boy will still care for her, and pre-marital sex hardly becomes satisfying. It certainly does not contribute to the fulfilling of her person. "Free love" is never true love. "Free love" is based on dishonesty. It ends in the girl's being deserted and with the feeling of having been used.

Some studies revealed that twice as many engagements have been broken when engaged couples have had intercourse. Many a young man has lost the desire to marry a girl who has been easy with him. Can it also be due to his loss of respect for her? A good marriage requires mutual respect. Is she the one to give strong moral values to a future family? If he misused sex before marriage, will he cheat with others after marriage? But he was as guilty as she. Is there a double standard? Yes and no. The young lady failed to play her role as God intended. God gave her inbuilt support. We have seen earlier that, at least naturally speaking, she was spiritually stronger than the boy, though he was physically stronger. Studies have further revealed that courtships which involved intercourse are more likely to end in divorce or in adultery after marriage. Unfaithfulness before marriage can lay the groundwork for unfaithfulness of another kind after marriage. God's laws are still the best and no new morality or changing standards of values of godless society will ever change what God has inbuilt into man.

The girl who is really intent on finding that ideal husband will need to be morally strong. She will need to develop the best that is in her and bring out the best that is in a young man. There is much truth to the statement that behind every good and successful man there is a good woman. "The hand that rocks the cradle rules the nation" is another axiom full of truth and meaning. When women lower their moral standards, the nation, the family is seriously weakened.

If the young ladies reading this book have understood that God has made the boy the aggressive sex, they will also watch their style of dress. The extremely short dress, the extremely tight clothing, the very low neck lines, the emphasis of breasts, all these may be a serious occasion of sin for a boy. The girl who deliberately dresses and acts in this manner to entice the boy is asking for trouble, sometimes more than she imagined. Modesty in dress and action is an essential Christian virtue. Also girls, don't try to mix dating and drink or you'll be handling a double intoxication. The boy's passions are already a problem. With liquor to accompany the sex appetite, you will be dealing with double trouble.

The girl at times may well have to decide that a change of dating pattern is essential. The time spent alone with the boy may have to be severely limited or dropped entirely. The need for group activities, spending time with other people, even with each other's parents or friends may be very essential. There are surely other things to do on the date than be alone and hold hands or go to the movies. Active participation in sports that are suitable for both may be in order; bowling, tennis, bicycling, etc. Sports can also bring a physical release of energy that might otherwise be directed to the immoral use of sex. A variety of encounters and situations will surely afford opportunities for growth and getting to know each other better under different circumstances. To grow in love, one must grow in knowledge.

What if some young girl reading this may have already violated her Christian values? Doubtlessly she experiences guilt. In a later chapter we shall deal with the sacrament of Penance (confession). But one thing is for certain. You cannot undo the past. If you have already made a serious mistake, you must not permit yourself to wallow in self-pity or refuse to forgive yourself. If you have repented and gone to God with a sorrowful heart, God has forgiven you. If God has forgiven you, you should be able to forgive yourself and leave the past behind. Bury it all in the Sacred Heart of Jesus. If you have not yet been to confession, approach the Sorrowful and Immaculate Heart of Mary for strength and guidance. She will surely lead you to the loving embrace of her divine Son.

"God is love and he who abides in love abides in God and God in him." Yes, love that is of the heart is true and deep. True love is never impure. It is noble and endearing and is never accompanied by feeling of guilt. I hope that the young ladies, the teenage girls, reading this book will have many happy dates ahead of them. You should pray each day that you may know your vocation in life. If marriage is your vocation from God, then pray daily that someday you will meet that special young man who will be your help to heaven, spreading truth, goodness, beauty and holiness in the lives of others, especially your future family.

A GIRL'S PRAYER BEFORE A DATE

Dear God, keep me in Your love on this date. May I return home closer to You because I have found a reflection of Your goodness in my friend.

Help me to be an attractive and interesting friend who is considerate of my companion. Grant us the grace to avoid temptations and be a source to each other in Christ of greater fulfillment of young love that is pure and wholesome. May our knowledge and tender love of each other grow in our hearts, if this be Your will. Amen.

QUESTIONS FOR DISCUSSION

1. Why is it important for boys and girls to understand that God has made them differently not only physically but emotionally?
2. Should a girl be insulted when a boy appears to make a pass at her? Explain your answer.
   a) How should she react if she is a good Christian young lady?
3. It is said that when a youthful couple fall into a sin of impurity the boy and girl are usually equally guilty. Comment on this.
4. Explain: The young man is *slow* to grow in a love that is deep and truly of the heart.
5. Explain: The good Christian boy highly respects the girl who requires modesty in word and action. Such a girl wins the *heart* of the boy.
6. Why is it wrong, if a boy says to a girl: "If you truly love me, you would be willing to go further"?
7. Psychologists, clergymen and counselors in general have been aware that unmarried young girls who have lost their virginity, even though pregnancy may not have resulted, seriously regret it afterwards. Why do they seriously regret their actions afterwards?

8. Does the couple unfaithful with each other before marriage stand a good chance of remaining faithful after marriage?

9. Why is "free love" called "dishonest" by the author?

10. Here is a young couple who because of circumstances and age, are justified in engaging in steady company keeping. They realize their temptations are becoming more difficult. How should they handle the problem to protect each other and keep their peace with God?

11. Discuss: God has given the young lady a role to assist the young man of her heart to keep his purity.

CHAPTER VII

SEX AND THE YOUNG MAN

Well, fellows, this chapter is especially for you. If you have been reading this book orderly and completely, by now you know sex involves much more than physical organs and movements. It involves deep inter-personal relationships. You realize by now that God has made boys and girls differently not only physically but emotionally. You know sex affects their very inner beings in great depth. God has made you boys physically stronger. You can use that strength for protection of others, including girls, to support a family some day, for personal skills and for recreation. You can also abuse your strength and energy and use it sinfully. In this chapter we shall speak bluntly but reverently.

There is much of the *Playboy* philosophy around today that worships the human body. It is ridiculous that even grown men are attracted by *Playboy* approaches. Some men remain adolescents all their lives. I do not mean to be critical of teenage boys. We do not expect complete maturity and emotional control at your age. But if you do not seek, with God's help, to mature and to learn how to control your sexual powers during adolescence, you will remain a child all your life even if you have an adult body. You are determined to become *men*. Much of the sex we see in movies, magazines and television is not only godless but extremely immature and selfish.

The fact that your young body already has the powers of fatherhood does not mean that you are yet a man. Manhood involves more than the power of fatherhood. Long before you are ready, emotionally and financially to be a father and a provider, your body is equipped sexually to reproduce. If marriage is your vocation from God, as it will be for most of you, there will be many times during your adult life when you must exercise self-control sexually. There will be times of illness for your spouse, even monthly periods. There will be times when in the months before and after the delivery of a child, your wife, the mother of your child, must be treated with extra care and tenderness which precludes sexual expressions in their full measure. There will be times when for various reasons, in the practice of responsible parenthood, you must exercise self-control.

Modern science is still striving to make progress to understand the fertility cycle better. As Catholic Christians we know that God forbids the use of artificial methods to limit or space children even within marriage. Progress is being made whereby husband and wife can better understand the fertile times and the times when nature (therefore God) provides that love-giving will not always result in life-giving. Mechanical methods, the use of pills as contraceptives, are ruled immoral by Christ's Church. It is true that the pill may be used in good conscience for serious reasons *which are not contraceptive.* When the pill is taken, *not* for contraceptive purposes, but to help correct a pathological condition, it may be permitted so long as there is evidence that it can help correct that health condition.

The point to make here is this. *If the teenage boy or the unmarried young man never learns self-control, even with himself, he is not going to make a good husband, a good father. He will not have a happy marriage.* Those years before marriage when the boy is sexually potent but forbidden to exercise such powers, are years of learning self-control, as well as years for seeking a marriage partner.

A good mother of a large family has shared with me this experience in her training of her teenage sons. She said, "After we had brought our last baby home and they had cuddled it and loved it, I said, 'I think we will give this one up for adoption.' My teenaged sons were stunned. 'But why?' they asked. 'We have so many and some people don't have any,' I replied. 'But you can't give your very own baby away!' they cried. 'I know,' I replied. 'And we won't. But just remember this: If you ever get a girl pregnant, *she* can take your baby away from you and give it away and you will never know what happened to it. Think about that!" That good mother said to me in conclusion. "The abstract idea of hell-fire didn't seem to scare them, but the thought of losing a baby they love seemed to get through to them."

The Catholic boy who practices his holy faith conscientiously may be able to practice control in his relationship with girls, but *alone with himself,* that is another matter. Masturbation may be a very real problem. Perhaps he got into the practice without at first realizing that it would be considered seriously sinful. Then someone tells him it is a mortal sin, and he is thoroughly shaken. In an earlier chapter we explained that the sex organs of the male body produce the seed of human life, or sperm, rapidly and in tremendous quantities. Sperm in the adolescent boy is plentiful and prolific. Nature had designed the sperm to be numerous so that when a man is married, there will be greater assurance that at least one sperm will be able to meet the female ovum and cause fertility. We see this often reflected in other areas of nature. Plants also produce abundant seeds, many of which never grow and result in new life. The seeds are plentiful to assure reproduction. Much of our food is the product of seeds such as from wheat, barley, oats.

The abundance of seeds produced in the boy's body is in part an explanation of why boys are more easily sexually aroused. The boy has a greater challenge in conquering his temptations resulting from sexual urges. He may be able to control his passions in relationship to girls, but he may seek solitary pleasure by the voluntary release of the seed when in private. This is called masturbation. It involves deliberate rubbing or pressures put upon the male organ to cause pleasure and release. In a former chapter we explained that nature itself will take care of the excessive seeds which the male body produces. The sperm will either be absorbed by the body in other ways or passed off during a noctural emission or wet dream while the boy is asleep. This is natural and good and the boy should in no way be concerned. If he awakens during the process, he should do nothing to help or to hinder what nature is accomplishing. He should strive not to consent to sexual pleasure in his mind although he cannot deny that some pleasure may be experienced in his body.

Where serious sin is involved is when he deliberately arouses himself and causes an ejaculation. In fact the boy who deliberately thinks of sex in order to cause an erection is doing serious wrong. If he looks at girls in an immoral way, or deliberately at pictures to cause sexual stimulation in himself, this is wrong. We again come back to the premise that sex is sacred and not just for fun.

What about the boy who finds girls attractive? Is that sinful? By no means. It is entirely natural and normal. The adolescent boy who does not find girls attractive would have something to worry about. It is abnormal for members of the *same* sex to be sexually attracted to each other in any great way. It would certainly be seriously sinful for members of the same sex to engage in sexual actions with each other.

There are borderline cases which will bother the good Catholic and Christian boy. There are times when he finds himself aroused sexually when he did *not deliberately* cause the erection by action or thought. He should have no worries about this. There is absolutely no sin involved. He should ignore it as best he can, change his activities if possible and surely strive to put his mind on wholesome subjects *not* related to sex.

There may be times when through necessary study about sex, the boy may find himself being aroused. If he does not deliberately and directly cause it, this should cause him no undue worry. If he does not give full consent, but perhaps experiences some pleasure, at the most he has probably been guilty of venial sin which does not destroy his share in the life of God. The wholesome dance, swimming, various recreations may accidentally have the effect of sexual stimulation which the boy never directly intends. If his reason for the normal and healthy occupation is not sexual arousal, the boy need have no qualms of conscience. It is true, on occasion he may give slight consent, but full and deliberate consent is always required for serious sin.

What about kissing? The kiss that is a gentle sign of affection for the unmarried is surely no sin. But there is again no reason which indicates that every time a boy and girl accompany one another on a date that a kiss must necessarily be a part of the date. A kiss is a sacred sign of affection and should never be used cheaply.

Passionate kissing would certainly be seriously sinful just as anything done deliberately to arouse the passions in the unmarried is wrong. A good boy may worry because, while *all he intended* was a kiss to show pure affection, nothing more, yet he did experience sexual arousal. Has he sinned seriously? No, he has not. He did not deliberately cause or intend the outcome. Experience will surely teach what must be avoided. The boy who finds himself becoming strongly sexually aroused in circumstances where normally he would not suspect he would be in a serious occasion of sin, would have the obligation, if possible, to remove himself from the circumstance. One must use common sense, of course, but still one must avoid occasions that place one in jeopardy.

It should be safe to say that, if you are in doubt whether you gave full consent to any sexual thought or action, you may presume that you gave no more than venial consent and did not lose the state of sanctifying grace. Please do *not* think of God as anxious to separate Himself from you. He rather seeks to keep you in grace.

What of jokes about sex? Surely one who tells jokes about sex with the intention to arouse himself or others is sinning seriously. It may prove a very difficult situation for a boy when someone starts telling dirty stories. He should immediately attempt to change the conversation. If he does not succeed, he should make a real effort not to consent to any pleasure which may result.

Masturbation could become a habit for a boy if he is not careful. While it is true that even the habit of self-abuse does not ruin a boy's health or harm him physically, yet it is a misuse of sex, a turning in on one's self. The habit must be brought under control. One may think he is the only boy in the world with this problem. This is not true. The problem is not unique. A person who has this problem is not abnormal or strange. He must, however, learn to control his passions and his sexual urges. He needs strong will power and he needs the help of God. God will not step in and perform any miracles. The boy himself must work at self-control. He should open his soul honestly to his confessor and not fear that the priest will condemn him. The priest will rather admire a boy who is humble, admits his weaknesses, and honestly wants to overcome his problem and live in God's holy grace. The boy with a problem of masturbation may even worry whether there is something about himself that gives away what is happening. He should not worry. There are *no* physical signs which identify you to others as a boy with such a problem.

That wise guy again who has no moral values and brags or lies about his sexual accomplishments is no help to the sincere boy who wants to control his sexual appetites. Such a braggart is dishonest. Some boys brag about the size of their sex organs. The size of sex organs is no indication of manliness or sexual powers. In a relaxed condition the penis is very small on the average boy or man, but the enlargement in length to 5 or 6 inches in hard erection is the norm. This is caused by blood flowing into the male organ. It returns to its normal small or relaxed condition as the blood flows back into the rest of the circulatory system.

The boy with a problem of deliberate masturbation should try to understand *why* he is led to this action. He will probably discover that it is associated with moods or feeling of depression and loneliness, a sense of failure. It is common that when one experiences unhappiness he will try to compensate by finding pleasure in some other manner. If one understands the cause, he is in a better position to know how to overcome the problem. God's help is essential but a boy must also use God's gifts to help himself.

"Charity" is part of the title of this book. It will be an important part of one's overcoming a serious problem of masturbation. You must learn not to be self-centered and self-pitying. You must become a generous person. You must learn charity by practice. Show special interest in others, beginning with members of your own family. In this way you will also develop confidence in yourself and develop a better and truer image of yourself. If you fall in a moment of weakness, don't get further depressed. Pick yourself up and answer God's call back to confession. Confess humbly that you sinned by impure actions when alone. State the number of times you deliberately sinned in this manner. Do not put off your confession thinking that it is as easy to confess that you sinned three times as twice, or six times as five. This is not being sincere with God or fair to yourself.

The devil will try saying to the boy with a problem of masturbation, "It's no use, you can't overcome it." Nonsense. Even if it takes a few years, you *can* overcome it. Thousands of boys before you were ever born overcame it. Thousands of good and manly fathers of families today once struggled against it as teenage boys, although they would no more like to talk about it than you would. The devil will try to get you so discouraged that you even give up the sacraments, or receive them in bad will, or finally give up going to Holy Mass, thinking, "It's no use. I'm going to hell anyway." Nonsense again. You're not essentially evil. You are basically a good young man. And God is infinitely good and merciful. And here you must remember that there are more laws than the sixth commandment. There are many elements of your life that are good and wholesome. God does not look *only* on your sexual failures. God looks upon your *total* life, most of which is pleasing to Him.

God created each one of you because He loves you. God understands sex because He made it. I have dealt with thousands of boys. I am firmly convinced that God is most gentle and understanding in every area of human failings but especially so in the area of sex because God understands the intensity of the sexual appetite. I believe our Divine Lord, Jesus Christ, is most merciful and gentle with the teenager who makes a mistake or is struggling to gain control of a new power that has arisen in his body. This is *not* to say that abuse is permissible. I am just saying that it is not a hopeless case and sexual failures, especially solitary acts, do not involve the greatest sins in the world. They may be serious and humiliating to the person thus involved, but the person who is dishonest in character, who is uncharitable and selfish as a rule of life in dealing with fellow man, has a far greater problem than the teenager who wants to be pure but occasionally falls in moments of weakness and frustration.

Jesus gave us the sacrament of Penance (confession) not because He was convinced that His followers would always be saints. Jesus gave us this sacrament of His mercy because He knew our weakness and wanted to give us all the spiritual help we would need to become saints. He wanted us to know with certainty that our sins were forgiven. We shall offer further suggestion about this beautiful sacrament in the next chapter when we again speak directly to *both* boys and girls.

What about going to confession before Holy

Communion? What if a boy has deliberately committed an act of masturbation? Could he go to Holy Communion without confession? Normally the answer is "No, he should go to confession first." It is possible to consider circumstances where the Church might consider him excused of confession first, but it would be a rare situation.

The boy of lax conscience could easily abuse what I am about to say here, but we have already concluded that any young person who reads this book orderly and completely is not one who is trying to cheat on God and be dishonest. I do think we should consider the exceptional case for the sake of the good conscience of sincere boys. It is true that the girl might find herself in this rare situation also, but the problems of boys, in this area at least, are more intense.

For the sake of example, let us say that on a Saturday night a boy was overcome with passion while trying to get to sleep. He was not on his guard as he should have been. It began by day dreaming, or should we say "night dreaming," only he was fully awake. He deliberately took pleasure alone in a sex act. The next morning the boy is reminded that this is a special occasion when the family will be going to Mass together and all will be receiving Holy Communion as a family unit. What to do? He has no opportunity to get a priest to hear his confession without exposing himself to family and friends. The boy feels bad not only because he did something very wrong before God and therefore should not receive Holy Communion, but he is sad because he thinks he offended God whom he greatly wants to receive. If he does not receive our Lord in Holy Communion, he will be saying, "Hey, mother and dad, family, I'm not going to Holy Communion with the rest of you because I committed a mortal sin." Now the Church expects us to reveal the secret sins of our soul to no one except the priest and then only under the sacramental keys of the confessional.

In the case outlined above, an *extreme case,* but one which could easily happen in some fashion or other, the Church would permit the boy to ask God for the gift of *perfect contrition* (explained further in next chapter). The boy is striving to live a good Catholic Christian life. He occasionally falls, even seriously. This was one of those occasions which he did not foresee. The boy stirs up dispositions of sorrow in his soul which are based on love of God. He is sorry not simply because he fears the punishments of God but because the all-good God was offended by his sin. The boy makes an act of perfect contrition with such sincere dispositions in his heart. He could then receive our Lord in Holy Communion worthily. We do not say the boy is receiving Jesus in mortal sin for it is believed that in such a situation God would forgive the mortal sin before actual confession and sacramental absolution. The boy (or girl) would *have* to confess the mortal sin in his next regular confession, however. Why? Because every mortal sin must be submitted to the sacramental keys of the confessional. In this case God acts in advance to His beautiful sacrament of mercy.

The conditions, to *summarize,* would have to be as follows before a teenager could ever go to Holy Communion after mortal sin without first going to confession. 1. There is an *urgent necessity* to go to Holy Communion on this particular occasion and if you don't receive, you would be publicly admitting you committed a mortal sin. 2. You have no opportunity to go to confession before Holy Communion and have had no opportunity to confess since falling into the sin. 3. You make an act of *perfect contrition* which is sorrow based on love of God Who has been offended by the sin. 4. You promise God you will confess the mortal sin the next time you go to confession.

Missing any one of the above conditions, it would be difficult to see how a teenager could in good conscience go to Holy Communion without confession first. I am convinced that no *sincere* Catholic teenager will abuse either sacrament.

The question has been asked whether a mortal sin is committed in each and every act of masturbation. We have already established that such acts done with *full deliberation* are seriously wrong. There are occasions where a boy could be aroused almost before he realized it. Any number of reasons or occasions could contribute to this, none of which he fully consented to. Then almost by impulse he finds that he has touched himself or experienced bodily movements and with little warning, the seed has been discharged. He acted more *impulsively* than with full deliberation. It would seem that there was no actual decision here on the part of the boy deliberately to offend God seriously. What he did may in itself have been wrong but with the sudden tension, or overwhelming pressure, perhaps much of it due to a biological condition at the time, or surprise, the condition for serious sin, *full consent,* may well have been lacking.

This again brings us back to a situation described formerly. If you are in *doubt* whether you have sinned seriously, you may presume that you did not sin more than venially. You need not stay away from Holy Communion because of a doubt.

To conclude this chapter, I think it essential to reflect on the role God has in mind for you boys with regard to girls. The added strength God has given your bodies means also that you are to be the protector of those weaker than you. Admittedly, girls and women may be able to endure more pain physically, yet normally the male sex is *physically* stronger. Any gift that God has given can be used for God's glory, according to His plan, or it can be used selfishly and abused. The same is true of the strength which boys have physically in their relationship to girls.

A boy should look upon girls with special respect and reverence. There is something of the goodness and holiness of the Blessed Virgin Mary that a boy should try to see reflected in girls. Scriptures have abundant evidence to show the workings of the Holy Spirit in the life of our Blessed Lady. Mary was completely open to the Holy Spirit. Everyone in the state of sanctifying grace is a temple of the Holy Spirit. This means both boys and girls. St. Paul reminds us of this indwelling of the Holy Spirit as in a temple. Scripture adds: "If anyone destroy the temple of God, him will God destroy because holy is the temple of God and this temple you are." This then is an indication of the reverence a boy should have for the body of a girl. The female body, while naturally attractive to the young man, must also be regarded as the temple of the Holy Spirit. The body is not an object for fun or jokes. It is a temple deserving of the greatest respect and reverence.

No boy has any right to intimate touches before marriage. Even engaged Christian couples whose commitment to each other in Christ has not yet been sealed in sacramental matrimony have no right to personal and private touches. The boy with non-Christian standards will joke about what he has or hopes to get. Notice we said "to get." Christian marriage is a generous *giving* and involves the total personality reaching to the depths of the soul.

When I was ordained as a Catholic priest, I was given in virtue of the sacrament of holy orders the right to touch and handle the Body of Jesus Christ in the Most Blessed Sacrament. Your Catholic faith tells you "that within the Holy Sacrament of the Eucharist, after the consecration of the bread and wine, our Lord Jesus Christ, true God and true Man, is really, truly and substantially contained under those outward appearances. In this way, the Savior in His humanity is present not only at the right hand of the Father according to the natural manner of existence, but also in the sacrament of the Eucharist by a mode of existence which we cannot express in words but which, with a mind illumined by faith, we can conceive, and must most firmly believe to be possible to God" (Pope Paul VI quoting the Council of Trent in his Encyclical Letter to the World on September 3, 1965, *The Mystery of Faith*).

The sacrament of matrimony gives the newly married husband and wife the right to touch and handle in most intimate ways the body of one's partner. The body is sacred and, in the sexual

embrace, a most personal physical union results
that is expressive of the union of persons. The
apostle Paul did not hesitate, under the inspiration of the Holy Spirit, to use this very union of
husband and wife as symbolic of the union of
Jesus Christ in and with His Church, His Mystical Body.

The union between Christ and the recipient
in Holy Communion is more than a physical
union. It is a Eucharistic union which strengthens
the union of Christ with the members of His
Church. The very reception of Jesus worthily in
Holy Communion serves not only to increase
God's life of sanctifying grace within us. It also
gives the recipient strength to handle concupis-
cence. We should not look for any automatic less-
ening of sexual desires as a result of receiving our
Lord in Holy Communion, but the Church does
teach that spiritual strength is thus received. In
the Eucharist, we come into direct contact with
the all holy Body of Jesus Christ and His glorified
soul. We go to Holy Communion not as a reward
for having been a saint but to help us become
saints.

The Catholic Christian boy will regard every
girl in some respect as a queen. His conversation,
his choice of words and actions in a girl's presence, will reflect his deep inner Christian reverence for her person. His added effort to be clean in
thought and conduct will show just what kind of
person he really is.

Nearly every girl is destined to be a mother. A
good Catholic boy wants to think of his mother as
a queen, a lady, worthy of great respect, a bearer
and nurse of life. A boy would never want to think

that his good mother had ever been a plaything. Any boy who makes a plaything of girls is ruining a girl destined to be the mother of a family some day. Every good Christian boy called to matrimony wants the mother of his children to be one who has always respected her own body, and one whose body was preserved holy for matrimony and motherhood and for the time when sex is truly sacred. The good Catholic young man thinks: "I must not desecrate what is holy and intended for holy purposes that reach into eternity. I must not be the cause of leading her and myself into sin."

With such a deep and Christian understanding of the opposite sex, which is really the complementary sex, a good Christian boy who fortifies himself with Christ in the sacraments will have no serious problems he cannot handle in the Lord.

A BOY'S PRAYER BEFORE A DATE

Dear God, You are love itself. Help me to share in Your love by the company I shall have in my friend on this date. I must be mindful that I am to be the protector in Your Name on this date. I must reflect Your goodness, Your strength that is wholesome, pure and enjoyable.

Help me to avoid deliberate temptations of places and circumstances. If my date is truly a Christian date, I should return home closer to You, dear God. May our knowledge and love of one another grow if this be Your Will. Amen.

QUESTIONS FOR DISCUSSION

1. Why did God make boys' bodies stronger physically?

    a) What are ways in which some boys abuse their physical strength?

2. Why is the expression "Playboy" used regarding those who do not mature in their concepts of sex?

3. Does a validly married man ever have to show control in the use of his sexual powers? Give some examples.

4. Can you name reasons why, in designing the human body, God placed the powers of fatherhood and the sexual drive in the boy's body years before he is normally ready to share such responsibilities maturely?

5. Why is the sexual drive in the young man much stronger than in the girl?

6. Why should the boy with a problem of masturbation not consider himself intrinsically evil or his cause hopeless?

7. Why is frequent confession strongly recommended for all youth, especially for the boy desirous of overcoming personal impurity?

8. Normally a boy who has been guilty of deliberate masturbation should repent and make a humble confession realizing the priest will understand with a sense of compassion. What about the unusual case when a boy finds his conscience troubled and it is assumed by the family that the *entire* family will be receiving our Lord in Holy Communion? (e.g. A funeral comes up of a close relative and your parents announce that "we should all go to Holy Communion at the funeral Mass.") The boy who

refused would be publicly exposing himself. He has no opportunity to get to a priest to hear his confession. The discussion should distinguish perfect and imperfect contrition and insist that this is an unusual case.

9. Is passionate kissing and embracing wrong for the unmarried?

10. If one is in doubt whether he has been guilty of serious sin, must he stay away from Holy Communion and go to confession first?

11. How should a boy regard every girl?

CHAPTER VIII

CONFESSION

There may be no particular difficulty experienced in confessing sins against charity, acts of unkindness, failures at generosity. Even admitting that one had deliberately consented to impure thoughts may cause no difficulty. But some find it most difficult to confess that one has deliberately been guilty of impure actions alone or with another. *They should not.* The person who has occasionally fallen into impure actions in moments of great temptation may well be living a better Christian life than some who have never failed in this manner. For many, such temptations are removed from their lives, but they are selfish in many other ways.

Before going further in our treatment of this beautiful sacrament of God's mercy, Penance, let me advise young people in this manner. In seeking a confessor, do not shop around for a priest who will be the easiest on you. Seek, if you must seek, that priest who will help you most. While every validly ordained priest has the powers of Jesus Christ to forgive sin in His Name, if you must seek a particular priest, seek that one who speaks to you most clearly for the Church in the Name of Jesus Christ.

I sincerely believe that there are an abundant number of understanding, compassionate and holy priests available. The sincere young person wants the priest confessor to give advice and encouragement to overcome sin. Just as our Lord refused to condemn the woman caught in the act of adultery when others would have stoned her to death, so the good priest will be kind and understanding while admonishing the young penitent to pray and work to sin no more.

This is what worries many a teenager and young adult. "But I know I will sin again." Well, we *should* fear we will sin again. The Bible tells us "to work out our salvation in fear in trembling." The fear of sinning again is not the same as *intending* to sin again. Experience may have taught us that we probably will sin again. But that does not exclude sorrow in our hearts here and now. And if we stay away from confession because we fear we will sin again, we surely will sin again frequently. To overcome sin, especially habits of sin, we need God's help and His sacraments.

The practice of averaging confession at least once a month is beautiful and good. The Church encourages *frequent* confession regardless of what the world says and regardless of what some Catholics may do. The teenager who falls into serious sin, however, should not wait until the month is up to go to confession. He or she ought to get to confession as soon as reasonably possible.

Teenagers often fear the priest will recognize them in the confessional. *Useless hours are spent in such fears.* If we talk in a whisper or a very low voice, the priest doubtlessly does not know who is confessing. I have been a priest in rural parishes for years at a time without recognizing who was going to confession. Even if the priest does recognize a particular penitent, why the fear? Consider why the man became a priest. If he is a good priest, the purpose was to help sinners glorify God and get to heaven. The sacrament of Penance is a very important part of this work. I find the greatest joy in hearing confessions because as a priest I meet Jesus constantly in the souls of young people and others. It is beautiful to witness the grace of God bringing these souls to confession and expressing their sincere desire to follow our Lord. There is perhaps no place where I experience spiritual fatherhood more than in the confessional where, as an instrument of Christ, I can increase or restore life to souls, God's own divine life.

The very Person of Jesus Christ is present and acts in the confessional. Why should we go to confession? Because Jesus Christ said so. He Himself gave us this sacrament. We should be grateful. The man who goes off by himself in private to pray and ask God's forgiveness has no sign from God that his sins are forgiven. But Catholic boys and girls who sorrowfully and sincerely confess their sins and receive the absolution of the priest, have a very clear and definite sign, established by Jesus Christ Himself. They can know that their sins are forgiven. No guess work here. You can read all about it in the twentieth chapter of St. John's Gospel. I urge each of you young readers to turn to that part of the Bible. There you will find these holy words of Jesus to the first priests:

"As the Father sent me, so am I sending you. Receive the Holy Spirit. For those whose sins you forgive, they are forgiven. For those whose sins you retain, they are retained" (Jn. 20:19-23). The five things necessary for the forgiveness of sins follow most logically.

1. Examine one's conscience.
2. Be sorry for our sins.
3. Have a firm purpose of amendment, the *intention,* that is, of working to avoid the sin in the future.
4. Be willing to perform the penance the priest gives us.
5. Tell our sins to the priest.

Every known mortal sin must be confessed. It has been said that we may deceive the priest but we cannot deceive the Holy Spirit. There is no reason to go to confession unless we are sincere and are convinced that this is a *real encounter with Jesus Christ.* The priest is the representative of Christ, but the very Person of Jesus works in and through the priest to forgive us.

Confession not only takes away sin, it gives grace to the soul. The sacraments, all of them, give us spiritual strength to fight temptations that will come up in the future. There is no magic to this. The sacraments do not mean that we will not be tempted again. Far from it. The very temptations can be a source of growing in grace. The teenager who has been severely tempted, but resisted, is a soldier truly tried in battle and proven worthy of Christ. The teenager who fell, but repented, is also a brave soldier of Christ. No quitter, this young person has risen like the prodigal son and returned to the Father's house. God the Father stands waiting with outstretched arms. When we return and ask for forgiveness, God takes us into His strong arms and bids the fatted calf be killed and prepared for the banquet. We are led to the Lord's banquet of Holy Communion where we eat His living Body, drink His Blood, and are restrengthened for our journey in this world which leads to heaven.

It was St. Catherine of Siena, the story goes, who experienced long and tortuous temptations against purity. The temptations, stronger than usual, lasted for hours. More than once she thought herself on the verge of falling but she persevered. Finally the temptations subsided. She called out, "Oh! Lord, where were You when I was being tempted?" Our Lord answered St. Catherine in this manner: "Catherine, when you were being tempted, I was in the midst of your heart. If I hadn't been here, do you think you could have resisted?"

So boys and girls, I beg you have no undue fears about this beautiful sacrament of Penance. The priest forgets your particular confession as quickly as he closes the confessional slide. In some cases young people may wish to go directly to the priest in his office to visit with him and discuss their personal problems. More power to you if you are convinced that will help. I've greatly admired young people, who, over the years, have been able to do so. I've never known such a soul ever to lose the precious gift of the Catholic faith. But for most, the private confessional will serve well.

There are pentitential services accompanied by songs, scriptural readings that are beautiful and prove helpful to many. But the important thing is faith in the reality of Christ Jesus to forgive in His presence in this sacrament. History not so far past, tells of men on the battlefield, kneeling or even lying beside the Catholic chaplain, confessing their sins in sorrow. They needed no particular ceremony or environment.

Consider the suffering of our Lord, behold the crucifix, all these can be helpful in stirring up in our souls sorrow for sin of whatever kind. There are two kinds of sorrow or contrition. One is *perfect* contrition and the other is *imperfect* contrition. Now both of these types of sorrow are valid and good. Imperfect sorrow does not mean that it is not good. It is just that imperfect sorrow is based more on fear of God's punishments. Perfect sorrow looks to God in love. The *motive* of perfect sorrow is that the all good and holy God has been offended by sin.

It is possible that God will forgive even a mortal sin before going to confession. If our sorrow is truly a *perfect* sorrow based on God's love, God will forgive the sin immediately if we also have the intention of confessing it the next time we go to confession. Now the Church says we must go to confession *before* Holy Communion if our conscience tells us we have committed mortal sin. We must have at least an imperfect sorrow to make a good confession. You can know whether you have an imperfect sorrow, that is, you can know whether you fear God's punishments and therefore intend to work to avoid the sin in the future. It isn't always easy to know whether your motive is perfect. The Church says we must have at least a moral certitude that we are in the state of sanctifying grace before we go to Holy Communion. Therefore, confession is required if we are aware of serious sin.

It takes three things to make a sin mortal. *First,* serious matter. *Second,* sufficient reflection that involves *full* consent of the will. *Third,* the serious act must be done with full knowledge. If any one of these three conditions is lacking, we have not committed a mortal sin.

In the case of the sexual appetite, the person may be severely tempted. But always remember this. *Temptation is no sin.* There may even follow physical pleasure after a temptation has taken hold. So long as consent is *not* given, there has been *no* sin. If slight but not full consent was given, one should not worry about more than venial sin. Again, we should not take venial sin casually. Any sin is an offense against God. But venial sin, small sin, does not destroy our share in God's life which is sanctifying grace. We are still God's friend. We may still go to Holy Communion. Frequent and deliberate venial sin, however, will weaken our wills and dispose us toward mortal sin. It is important that we struggle against all sin.

In concluding this chapter, let me encourage you again to make frequent use of the sacrament of Penance. This is what the Church wants. Don't wait until you feel you must go. You meet Christ in this sacrament every time. Meet Him there frequently. Open your hearts and souls in sincerity, humility, honesty. Forget about the particular man who is the priest. Think essentially about

Jesus Christ. *He is the Priest.* He is there waiting for you in love and mercy. And He has said, as the Bible has recorded, "there is more joy in heaven over one sinner doing penance than over 99 just men who have no need of repentance." Jesus has told us that the angels in heaven rejoice at the return of a sinner.

We are all sinners. The apostle of love in Sacred Scripture has said that anyone who claims he is not a sinner is a liar. Now, we may not all be guilty of the same kinds of sins, but we all sin occasionally. The sacrament of penance gives grace to the soul as well as the forgiveness of sin. From the positive values alone, frequent confession should be a part of the life of every good Catholic.

QUESTIONS FOR DISCUSSION

1. Discuss: A person who has sinned seriously against charity finds no difficulty in confessing such a sin. He finds it much more difficult to confess a sin against purity. Should one really hesitate or delay confession for the latter reason?
2. Discuss: An individual avoids confession because he fears he will sin again in the same way.
3. Explain the Catholic teaching that the very Person of Jesus Christ is present and acts in the confessional. How is this possible?
4. Is there evidence in the Bible that Jesus instituted a special sacrament for the forgiveness of sin?
     a) Where? What did Jesus say?

5. What are the five things necessary to make a good confession?

   a) Explain each of them briefly.

6. Besides the forgiveness of sin, what are the positive benefits of going to this special sacrament of forgiveness, called "Penance"?

7. Discuss: Here is an individual who shops around for a priest who is easy on him, doesn't say much, or seems to let one off easy even when he has been guilty of serious sin. Should the individual rather seek a priest who will encourage one to use God's graces and self-help to overcome sinful habits?

8. What are the three things necessary to make a sin mortal?

9. Discuss: Temptation in itself is no sin. In fact, temptation can be a time for growth in grace and the love of God.

10. Discuss the two types of sorrow.

    a) Which type is necessary to make a good confession?

11. How often should a sincere Catholic young man or woman desirous of growth in holiness participate in the sacrament of Penance?

CHAPTER IX

THE CATHOLIC CHURCH AND THE SEXUAL REVOLUTION

There is one thing I have never bought. It is this. That modern young people are essentially permissive. *They are not.* I find that young people are morally good and are in search of the real Jesus of the Gospels. Jesus was and is a real man. Now Jesus is, of course, the risen and glorified Savior. He once walked the dusty roads of Palestine. He lived on our earth. Jesus experienced the same human emotions as we do. He ate, slept. wept, grew in body and human experiences. He had sorrow. He feared and He loved as a man, with the deeper reality of divine love blended with the fullness of humanity.

There is much in the world today that is permissive, that is, not in accord with Christian morality. I do *not* think we can essentially blame it on the young people. They did not make the social conditions which represent this world. I have often said that where young people are confused and have serious problems regarding the faith, it is often because older people have scandalized them or have not correctly communicated the authenticity of the fullness of the faith of Jesus Christ. Ultimately, of course, the faith means the embracing of Jesus Christ and all His teachings. Jesus is the Crucified Christ. Even at His birth, the shadow of the Cross fell across the manger. He was born in poverty, in a place meant for animals, rejected by the world, no room for Him in the inn. His birth became the occasion for a mad king to seek Him out when the Magi came searching for the Christ Child after following the star. When Herod did not succeed, he ordered the slaughter of the innocent babes, all children two years of age and younger, attempting to murder the Christ Child. It was really an attempt to murder the source of his guilty conscience and the threat to his worldly powers and pleasures.

We have indicated more than once in this book that the whole of Christian faith and morality is not the obeying of the sixth commandment only, although that which concerns sexual morality can be a most difficult part of morality. It is said that as a result of the effects of Original Sin committed by our first parents, Adam and Eve, whereby the intellect was darkened and the will weakened, one of the greatest upsets in human nature has been in the area of sexuality. In this area, man's reason and his will power frequently do not show proper control and balance. Few will deny the truth of this.

Some may ridicule the approved apparitions of the Mother of God at Fatima, Portugal, in 1917 in which she showed the children a terrible vision of hell and also said, "more souls go to hell because of sins against the flesh than for any other reason," but our Blessed Mother was not the first to indicate that. St. Alphonsus said that there are more souls in hell because of the violation of the virtue of chastity than for any other reason. St. Jerome said that nine out of ten who are in hell are there because of sex sins. Now I don't know that St. Alphonsus and St. Jerome went down into hell and made a scientific investigation, but it surely reflects, to say the least, what learned and holy men, those experienced with souls and human nature, have concluded regarding the difficult virtue of chastity.

Spiritual things become distasteful to the impure man. Violation of holy purity will often result in the loss of faith, the neglect of the sacraments of Penance and Holy Communion and the neglect of prayer and the Mass. We may also say that the neglect of the sacraments, of prayer and the Sacrifice of the Mass will result in the failure, especially for the young, to remain pure. A further purpose of this book has been to relate that the fullness of our holy Catholic Christian faith must be reflected upon and *lived* to be authentic.

My experience has been that most youth and young adults, when they have the Catholic faith and its morals adequately explained to them, do respond and accept it beautifully; yet, where there are difficulties in accepting the official Catholic teachings on sexual morality, it is because the person is not understanding, considering, accepting his *holy faith in its fullness*. He is isolating doctrines and disciplines. He is separating the Church from Christ Jesus. He considers a doctrine a cold abstraction, not a truth taught by

Jesus, and he fails to see law as the will of God. He does not really understand that the Church is Christ Jesus, His Mystical Body, and that we are the People of God, joined as branches to the Vine which is Christ. He looks at the Church as a mere natural organization.

I have dealt with thousands of souls in different places and in my parish. Writing has brought me into contact with many thousands more people of all ages on this continent and beyond. There are those occasional Catholics who will even come to the sacraments in a spirit which does not reveal the humility needed to receive the sacraments worthily. Their spirit is one of contempt. They are willing to blame the Pope, the bishops, the teaching Church for their problems. They will say such things as the following: "I believe in God. I believe in Jesus. It is just some things about the Church I can't accept. After all, a handful of people determine for millions of others what is right and wrong. They tell us not to practice artificial birth control. They don't have to support those children. The people who have to support them should be permitted to decide what is right and what is wrong. The Pope or bishops don't know what it is to be in love. I have done such and such but I don't believe it is a sin."

The big question to such an attitude is this. If they *honestly* don't consider it a sin, then why are they so concerned? Why the upset? The point is that these people are not really being *honest*. *Honesty* is a much needed virtue today along with purity. If one cannot really be honest within his own conscience he is surely going to find it difficult to be honest with God and fellow man.

I am convinced that people who say they cannot understand the teachings of the Church on sexual morality or cannot accept the official teachings of the Church, do not in fact understand the real nature of the Church. Some are saying: "People are the Church. We are all the Church, just as much as the Pope and bishops. The Holy Spirit works in the laity as well as in the hierarchy." You see, young people, a half truth is often more dangerous than no truth. It is true that all the people make up the Church. It is true that the Holy Spirit dwells in all the people who are in the state of sanctifying grace. The Spirit does work within us all, the Pope, the college of the world's bishops, priests, religious and all baptized souls. But the Holy Spirit does not work in all of us in the same way or to the same degree.

The people are the Church. But not all the people are the *head* of the Church. Even the Pope as visible head of the Church is not the invisible head. The invisible head of the Church is Jesus Christ, Truth Itself. Truth is unchangeable. Truth is one. You cannot have objective truth when you have contradictions about the same thing, at the same time, in the same respect. Two contradicting answers about the same thing cannot both be right. One answer may be only an opinion. In fact, both answers may be only opinions. But in objective truth, only one answer is the true answer. Jesus did not set up His Church to issue mere opinions, but to speak with authority. "He who hears you, hears Me," Jesus said to the first college of bishops, the apostles. The Bible says the Church is to have *one faith* as there is *one* Lord. The Pope as visible head of the Church is answerable to the invisible Head, Jesus Christ. Our divine Lord keeps the Church, speaking through the Pope and the college of bishops, in the truth through the action of the Holy Spirit.

If each individual was infallibly guided by the Holy Spirit, Who is the "Spirit of Truth," then every individual Christian should be in agreement because *truth is one.* Of the 400 or more Churches in the world, obviously millions of Christians disagree with each other on the same points. All cannot be true. All cannot be the head. God does not contradict Himself.

Christians who disagree with the official Catholic position on faith and morals are not insincere. I once questioned a large group of teenagers in this manner. "What is truth?" Most answered that truth was sincerity. They went on to explain that if you really believed in something, that made it true. I asked them about the man who was color blind and really believed that red was green. Would that make red green? Or the person who occasionally was subject to double vision and glanced into the next room where there was a table with five apples. She relates in all sincerity that there are ten apples on that table in the next room. She is sincere. Does she have the correct or truthful answer? Some will answer, "To her, yes." Ah! but that is only her opinion. In reality, in objective reality, are there five or are there ten apples on the table?

God set up a Church. How did He set it up? Did Jesus Christ, God become man, say, "Now I'm writing a Bible for each one of you to interpret for yourselves. I'll give each of you the Holy Spirit to interpret it correctly. You need no authority over you; you are all equal in interpreting my voice for yourselves on faith and morals." Is that what Jesus said? Is that what the Church is? *By no means.*

Even contemporaries of Jesus noticed how He spoke definitely and with authority. This was a distinctive mark about Jesus. He did not utter mere opinions like other teachers of His day. People were amazed at His teachings and said, "Why this man speaks with authority." Before His ascension Jesus told His apostles, "All authority in heaven and on earth has been given to me. Go, therefore, make disciples of all the nations; baptize them in the name of the Father and of the Son and of the Holy Spirit, and teach them to observe all the commands I gave you. And know that I am with you always; yes, to the end of time" (Mt. 28:18-20).

It has been objected that we only have to listen to the magisterium (Pope and bishops united with and under the teaching authority of the Pope) when the Pope issues a definite infallible declaration. This is not the authentic teaching of the Church. The Church has taught in the past and repeated at the second Council of the Vatican, which adjourned on December 8, 1965, that we must give *religious assent of will and mind* to the constant teachings of the Church, even the ordinary day-to-day teachings.

"Ex cathedra," meaning from the chair, is an expression used to explain definitive statement by the Pope on faith or morals which must be accepted by all Catholic people. The Church does not frequently issue "ex cathedra" pronouncements. But there is still that constant teaching day after

day, year after year, which is part of the deposit of faith given by Christ to His apostles, which we must believe and endeavor to live by.

Unfortunately, few have read the 16 documents of Vatican II. Permit me to quote for you here from the *Dogmatic Constitution on the Church.* "This religious submission of will and of mind must be shown in a special way to the authentic teaching authority of the Roman Pontiff, even when he is not speaking ex cathedra. That is, it must be shown in such a way that his supreme magisterium is acknowledged with reverence, the judgments made by him are sincerely adhered to, according to his manifest mind and will. His mind and will in the matter may be known chiefly either from the character of the documents, from his frequent repetition of the same doctrine, or from his manner of speaking."

The same document of the Vatican II Council continues: "Although the individual bishops do not enjoy the prerogative of infallibility, they can nevertheless proclaim Christ's doctrine infallibly. This is so, even when they are dispersed around the world, provided that while maintaining the bond of unity among themselves and with Peter's successor, and while teaching authentically on a matter of faith or morals, they concur in a single viewpoint as the one which must be held conclusively. This authority is even more clearly verified when, gathered together in an ecumenical council, they are teachers and judges of faith and morals for the universal Church. Their definitions must be adhered to with the submission of faith.

"This infallibility with which the divine Redeemer willed His Church to be endowed in defining a doctrine of faith and morals extends as far as extends the deposit of divine revelation, which must be religiously guarded and faithfully expounded. This is the infallibility which the Roman Pontiff, the head of the college of bishops, enjoys in virtue of his office, when, as the supreme shepherd and teacher of all the faithful, who confirms his brethren in their faith (cf. Lk. 22:32), he proclaims by a definitive act some doctrine of faith or morals. Therefore his definitions, of themselves, and not from the consent of the Church, are justly styled irreformable, for they are pronounced with the assistance of the Holy Spirit, an assistance promised to him in blessed Peter. Therefore, they need no approval of others, nor do they allow an appeal to any other judgment. For then the Roman Pontiff is not pronouncing judgment as a private person. Rather, as the supreme teacher of the universal Church, as one in whom the charism of the infallibility of the Church herself is individually present, he is expounding or defending a doctrine of Catholic faith."

I find it then, young people, impossible to understand the statement of anyone who would consider himself a Catholic and say, "I believe in Jesus, (or) I believe in the Church, there are just things about it I can't accept." Ask what, and usually it concerns accepting the authority of the Church on sexual morality before or after marriage. They will not say, "I reject the authority of the Church," but that is what they are doing. They name the things which they find difficult to observe and which cost them sacrifice. Things that are no problem to them, they say they accept. One wonders about faith and honesty.

As for the "handful of people deciding for millions," we have already explained that Jesus has given His Church the *Holy Spirit* to teach us faith and morals through the Pope and college of bishops, and not through the entire Church. Such a person would do well to read the twelfth chapter of First Corinthians where the Apostle Paul explains that the Church as the Mystical Body of Christ is one body with many members, the various parts having various functions. The Apostle says: "Now you together are Christ's body; but each of you is a different part of it. In the Church, God has given the first place to apostles, the second to prophets, the third to teachers. . . ." The Apostle concludes with telling us: "Be ambitious for the higher gifts. And I am going to show you a way that is better than any of them." He then begins a new chapter on the better way which consists of the *charity* we spoke of in Chapter II. "If I have all the eloquence of men or of angels, but speak without love, I am simply a gong booming or a cymbal clashing."

The point the Apostle makes here is that if we truly have Christian charity, we will rejoice in the truth, be willing to sacrifice and not be selfish. Charity does not seek self-pleasure "but delights in the truth." Charity is willing "to endure whatever comes," even when the truth hurts. The man who does not have charity will rather rely on scientific technology. He will say, "If we have the 'know-how' to avoid conception, then let us use sex for fun." It never occurs to him that what is legal is not necessarily morally right and that sacrifice and self denial is often a part of the Christian life. Jesus taught this profoundly by His death on the Cross with sacrifice already fore-shadowed in His birth.

That there are many good young people, loyal to the Church, understanding of its teachings, is evidenced by the 17-year-old senior of a public high school in St. Paul, Minnesota, whom I'll per-mit to finish this chapter for me. There are thou-sands of Catholic teenagers in the United States or Canada who could have done as well but we shall permit Jeff Wood to serve as an example in this case. He wrote the article below in response to a guest speaker from Planned Parenthood.

The Sexual Revolution
In The United States

Seventy-five years ago in our Country, the word "sex" was hardly a part of the American vo-cabulary; and probably those who used it were looked down upon by the rest of society as being immoral or even sinful. Along with this word "sex," obscene magazines, lewd films, topless bars, artificial birth control, and abortion were all steeped in obscurity. One would have spent a great deal of time searching to find any one of these evils about him. As little as possible was said in regard to sex. Sex education was strictly limited to what was said between parent and child. Obviously little needed to be said; children were being born. Generally, sex remained as it had in the past: not to be spoken of. It retained its dignity as a sacred act instituted by the Creator, and any attempt to exploit it was condemned and suppressed on all sides as being a grave sacrilege.

Seventy-five years later however, in brisk contrast, sex has become an obsession of society. Frank Sheed, in his Society and Sanity, puts it very bluntly:

"The typical modern man practically never thinks about sex.

"He dreams of it, of course, by day and by night; he craves for it; he pictures it, is stimulated or depressed by it, drools over it. But this frothing, steaming activity is not thinking, picturing is not thinking, craving is not thinking, dreaming is not thinking. . . ."

The attempt that was made in society several years ago to become more open and frank about sex was catastrophic. It was met with a flood of gross abuses of what sex really is. Filthy magazines, exploitive literature, pornographic movies, general promiscuity by young and old alike, moral-less sex-education classes in public institutions, and frightening marital instability all marched proudly onto the American scene. Soon it even became the "in thing" for teenagers to experiment with sexual intercourse outside of marriage, and the great moral decline that has plagued our Country in recent years was given its real genesis.

The mistakes soon began to appear. Unwanted children by the thousands needed to be coped with; a new problem had arisen for society to deal with. Inevitably, artificial methods of birth control were introduced on a large scale to prevent the continuance of the problem. Because the sexual act had lost the essential parts of its sacred meaning — the true love between two persons culminating with the procreation of children — it became merely an act of pleasure and passion. Man became animalistic in his desire to experience sex; once a being with a backbone and the ability to reason, he now became a mere jellyfish in his attempt to deal with sexual passions. The new artificial birth control afforded him an easy ride with no strings attached (at least no children), and contraception became the welcomed third partner in the beds of millions throughout the Country.

Sadly enough, a large number of Christian churches abandoned their once morally sound principles and gave their support to the new immorality. They actually, for the first time in their history, allowed the use of artificial birth-control methods which before had either been strictly off-limits or at least understood to be so. And so it is not surprising that a vast number of people in our Nation have little or no guilt feelings about the use of the sex act before or outside of marriage. The pill and contraceptives are used without second thoughts by millions.

The interference of humans in God's plan for creation had become all too common a practice. Abortion, the destruction of an already conceived life, inevitably began to follow. The abortionists (those who supported abortion) reached their great triumph on Jan. 22nd, 1973, when the court of the same government that had made the destruction of a Bald Eagle's eggs a Federal offense made it legal to remove the fetus of an unborn human child from its mother's womb to be dropped in a bucket to wither and die. This clearly illustrated how man had put a relative value on human life — something that in my estimation

can never be done. Regardless of how close to ex-
tinction any mere animal may be, human life is
drastically more precious, and there must be leg-
islation to protect and preserve it first and foremost.

Nevertheless, the annual mass slaughter of
nearly two million innocent human beings was
given an amen by the highest court in our Land.
In the name of individual freedom, the destruction of human life became the right of each individual — except the individual being destroyed.

The warm welcome that has been given to
Planned Parenthood and other similar organizations in the United States has helped to worsen
the situation. These organizations are very un-
realistic in their dealing with the problems of
today. They see pollution and overcrowded cities
and automatically hit the panic button by declaring that the population is exploding and must be
drastically reduced. They are working backwards
to solve the environmental problems, and have ig-
nored the many real possibilities for pollution
control and city planning that are by far much
more effective and permanent solutions than
birth control and family planning.

Our age has seen a great reversal in society's
outlook on sex. Once seldom discussed, it it now
spoken of in the same shameful breath as is filth
and obscenity. This is only a result of its many
abuses in the past years. And today, instead of society frowning down upon those who abuse sex, it
has turned against the people who have withstood
moral decay and who still cling to God-given principles, laughing and scoffing at them being stuffy,
old-time fools. The United States of America is

rapidly deserting its precious Judaeo-Christian heritage to become one of the most pagan countries in the world — a Nation submerged in sexual corruption and drastic moral decline. It really makes me wonder if trying to make "sex" a little more relevant wasn't the biggest mistake ever made in the history of our Nation. — *Jeff Wood*

QUESTIONS FOR DISCUSSION
  1. Do you agree with the author that, in general, young people today are not essentially permissive?
  2. What is meant by the statement: "The whole of Christian faith and morality is not found in the obeying of only the sixth commandment."
  3. Spiritual writers have often held that more souls go to hell because of sins against the flesh (impurity) than for any other reason. Why do you think this has commonly been held?
  4. What are some other serious sins, besides impurity, which people may commonly be guilty of and which they regard too lightly?
  5. What about the person who has been guilty of serious sin and comes to confession with a spirit of contempt for Church authority and teachings on morality?
  6. Explain: Some people find it difficult to be honest with God and with oneself.
  7. Discuss: "All the People are the Church."
     a) Give a true explanation of how this can be correctly used.
     b) Explain how some can abuse this statement to disregard the authority of the Pope and college of bishops.

8. Briefly explain the Church's nature as the Mystical Body of Christ.

9. What was the thing the contemporaries of the historical Jesus especially noticed about His teachings?

10. Explain what is meant by an "ex cathedra" teaching of the Church.

11. Using the direct quotations from Vatican Council II in this chapter, or by going directly to the documents of Vatican II, explain how the sincere Catholic must observe not only "ex cathedra" pronouncements of the Church but ordinary day-to-day teachings constantly presented by the Church.

12. Explain what is meant by the Holy Spirit as the *Soul* of the Church and *Spirit of Truth*.

13. Did Jesus teach us to follow the easiest course if we have the technology to do so?

14. Why is penance (the cross) essential to authentic Catholic Christian life?
    a) Explain why the Church, as Jesus, commands regular penance in our lives.
    b) How can self denial be related to a life of purity?

15. Briefly discuss the sexual revolution that has taken place in the United States.

CHAPTER X

THE HOLY FAMILY AND THE ADOLESCENT CHRIST

I have tried to write this book like an informal visit with you young people who are the hope of the Church tomorrow. I have tried to speak plainly and clearly on the faith and moral teachings of the Church. I have tried to be neither prudish nor irreverent in handling what I consider a sacred subject, sex. Because I have spoken definitely on the moral aspects of human sexuality, there will be those who will point a finger saying "triumphalism." My goal, however, has been to please God and assure your own joy in time and triumph in eternity.

It becomes a little difficult to underscore what some mean by "triumphalism." Triumphant refers, according to Webster's Dictionary, to "conquering, victorious." Triumph has a second meaning, "to celebrate victory or success boastfully or exultingly." It has been said that since Vatican II there is no honest room for triumphalism in the Church and that it is against "the spirit of the Council." But then a lot of things have been said to be "according to the spirit of Vatican II" which can in no way be found in the Council documents.

It appears to some that to speak clearly and to quote the authority of the Church is to be guilty of "triumphalism" and self righteousness. Some have so feared being accused of triumphalism that they have hesitated to quote the official doctrines of faith and morals of our holy Church. They have hesitated to speak of the Catholic Church as being that Apostolic Church founded by Jesus Christ and in possession of the fullness of the true faith through the power of the Holy Spirit. Sometimes it is stated in indirect ways. "Religion should cause more questions than it presents answers. . . . Our faith should be one of continuous searching but never arriving at any definite conclusions. . . . We must never force our values on others. Youth must decide for themselves what values they desire and what they consider good faith." It is my contention that such an approach to our holy faith is largely responsible for disillusioning many youth. Such an approach is not the approach of the Catholic Church. Of course we may not *force* our values on others, but true Christian values *correctly communicated* will reveal their own attractiveness and be sought after by idealistic youth, even at the cost of great personal sacrifice.

I consider doctrines to be truths about the Person I love. That Person is the God-Man, Jesus Christ, Who is the *Way* to God the Father. He is also the *Truth* and the *Life*. One cannot love a person he does not know. The doctrines of the

Church are truths about Jesus. Doctrines bring us knowledge about Jesus. We get to know individuals we do not encounter physically by reading about them, listening to others speak about them. This is the function of the doctrines of the Church. They bring knowledge about Jesus. We then encounter the very Person of Jesus Christ spiritually. When we respond in faith, hope and love, Jesus becomes real and present to us. He lives in our souls by grace. Then with St. Paul the apostle, each one of us can say, "For me to live is Christ. . . . It is now no longer I who live, but Christ Who lives in me."

Sanctifying grace is a sharing in the very life of God. St. Peter in Scripture speaks of sanctifying grace as making us "partakers of the divine nature." By grace we are lifted above the mere nature of men. While remaining ourselves, we still *share* in the very nature, the very life of God. St. Catherine of Siena could behold by imagery a soul in the state of grace and think she was seeing God Himself. The brightness, the light, the beauty that shone from the soul was so magnificent that the saint said, "If I did not know there was only one God, I would have thought I was seeing another."

The angel that was with her explained it was the grace of God in that soul that made it so beautiful. And to think that we can grow and grow in this grace so that one day in heaven we can live the God-life more intensely for all eternity. Our life of heaven will not be merely for our own enjoyment and happiness but also to be able to glorify God, the entire Blessed Trinity, more fully and render God the glory that is His due, and fulfill the purpose of our creation. That will be when we are part of the Church triumphant.

Christ said, "I am the light of the world." If we cannot know doctrines of faith and morals clearly, if we must remain in darkness about what is true faith and what is right and wrong, then we are like men without a Savior and without Christ Jesus Who said, "I am the way, the truth and the life." I am reminded of what we sing in the *Adeste Fideles* every Christmas season, "Oh come, all ye faithful, joyful and *triumphant.*" I do not think it is self righteousness to believe, as we should, that Jesus established a Church to speak clearly, definitely with authority as to what is true faith and what is right moral. The credit goes, not to self, but to God and to His Third Person, the Holy Spirit, Spirit of Truth. In this way, the voice of the Church is the voice of Jesus Christ. No man gets the credit; only God does.

Jesus spoke as One having authority. In this manner He commissioned His holy Church to teach, "knowing that I am with you all days even unto the end of the world." Since Jesus founded a Church with infallible authority, I have attempted to write this book in harmony with the constant teaching authority of Jesus Christ in His Church. I have not hesitated to call sin, sin. I have hoped that I have presented at the same time our God in Christ Jesus as a loving God. We must avoid any terrible ideas that God is a tyrant in heaven, ready to pounce upon us if we make the slightest mistake. We must always remember the infinite ocean of mercy that is Jesus Christ. We must be convinced that God is a loving Father, kind, considerate, always seeking to bestow His inexhaustible love upon us. As Scripture tells us, God wills not the death of the sinner, but his salvation. Mortal sin is not an utterly hopeless situation. God does not let us fall easily into sin at the slightest mistake.

I do believe at the same time that God has given us much light in giving us His Son, Jesus Christ, to be not only our Savior but our very Brother. In Jesus we come so close to God. By becoming one in Jesus, we become one with God the Father in the unity of the Holy Spirit. By being in the *state of grace,* the entire Blessed Trinity dwells in our souls. We need not then pray to a God in a far-off heaven, *He lives within us.*

Holy Mother Church has approved of prayers such as the following and bestowed its indulgenced blessing upon such aspirations:

"O Most Holy Trinity, I adore You Who are dwelling by your grace within my soul.

"O Most Holy Trinity, Who are dwelling by your grace within my soul, make me love you more and more.

"O Most Holy Trinity, Who are dwelling by your grace within my soul, sanctify me more and more."

The human soul is a spirit and therefore exists whole and entire in *every part* of the human body. Body and soul are fused as one making up the person which is myself. Sister Elizabeth of the Blessed Trinity used to say, "I have found my heaven on earth for heaven is where God is and God is in my soul." With this realization of our intimate union with God, we can pray in reverence the *Morning Offering,* making of every prayer, work, joy and suffering of each day an act of love in union with the Sacred Heart of Jesus and through our devotion, too, to the Immaculate Heart of Mary.

Then too, the beautiful powers of sex developing within the human body can all be seen as part of God's beautiful design and goodness. Temptations to abuse these powers can be accepted as so many opportunities to show our great love for Jesus and to resist them because we love God so much. One who is never tempted does not have the opportunity to show his love for God under fire. Remember what we said: "A temptation in itself is never a sin." It is an opportunity to grow in God's grace.

Generosity is the key to success in handling our sexual powers as God intended. Unselfishness in the home, e.g. consideration for the meals mother cooks, being helpful to younger members of the family, respectful to older members and making dad feel loved and needed because he really is. Don't take him for granted. From the home, *where charity begins,* our unselfish spirits must expand to our church activities, our school programs, our entire community.

Our Blessed Mother Mary is our ideal as the perfect Christian. She is the Mother of the Church but also the perfect model of the Church. Whom would you take as the perfect model of being a Christian? Usually, presented that question in another context, young people will answer, "Jesus Christ." But did Jesus have faith? The God-Man could hardly have had faith upon earth, being God Himself in His very Person. St. Thomas Aquinas held that the soul of Jesus always beheld the beatific vision. His soul always beheld the infinite essence of the Blessed Trinity. He was the Second Person of the Most Blessed Trinity. He was not a human *person*, though He did have a human *nature*. Mary is truly the Mother of God because the Son she conceived, bore and nursed, was truly the Second Person of the Blessed Trinity, eternal in His Person, but born in time through the human nature He took of Mary.

Mary had to *believe* God's Word. The Bible makes various references that Mary pondered God's Word in her heart. Mary is the *Mother* of the Son. She is the *Daughter* of God the Father. Mary is the *Spouse* of the Holy Spirit. Because of culture and circumstances when Mary lived upon earth, Jewish girls matured early, both physically and mentally. When she was in her teens, Mary conceived the Christ Child by the overshadowing of the Holy Spirit. She was not an ignorant young lady by any means. The Church calls her "the Seat of Wisdom." When the Angel Gabriel announced to Mary that it was the will of God she become the mother of the Messiah, Mary asked about her vow of virginity. She surely knew the sacredness of the marital embrace and inquired, "But how can this come about, since I am a virgin?" Some translators have rendered it, ". . . because I do not know man" (Luke 1:26-38).

As our Blessed Lady nursed the Christ Child, watched Him grow physically and in human experiences, Mary constantly had to have *faith* that this Son of hers was actually also the Son of God. Think of the faith she had to have when she finally witnessed Jesus crucified on Calvary. And what about Joseph, the true husband of Mary and the foster father of our Lord, Jesus Christ? His faith surely had to be the greatest after Mary's. We are too inclined to forget about St. Joseph.

I am happy that most artists in more recent years render Joseph as a young man. He has been falsely pictured as an aged man, long beard, humped over, one in whom the energy of passion could hardly have the strength to arise. Rather, Joseph was a young man, full of energy, virile, very capable of every human expression of love. He was the protector of the Holy Family and has been named the Protector of the Universal Church. He who protected both the Head of the Church and the Mother of the Church is surely, after Christ, a most perfect model of manhood.

Joseph knew Mary was with child. He also knew he was not the father of the Child Mary was carrying. But he trusted Mary. Joseph had to have great faith too, both in Mary and in the Child she bore as the Son of God. It is gradually revealed to Joseph that the Father of this Child is the First Person of the Blessed Trinity, and that the Holy Spirit has also chosen Mary as His Spouse. Contemplate all this and you will get some idea of the greatness and holiness of St. Joseph. He too had sacrificed his sexual powers for a higher good, not because sex is evil, but for the kingdom of God. This is in evidence by the question Mary asks of the Angel. Obviously, for the love of God, both Mary and Joseph had pledged to sacrifice their powers of sex. They were a husband and wife whose love was so noble, so great, so holy, so spiritual, that it did not need the sexual embrace.

The fact that Mary and Joseph lived continuously in a state of virginity in no way reflects evil upon the normal married state which does involve the holiness of the sexual embrace. But the *Holy Family* of Jesus, Mary and Joseph is a model for everyone and every family. The young ladies who are virgins can find in this family a model in Mary. The *accused* young lady can look to Mary for comfort. Mary spent time in suffering without being able to reveal the facts to Joseph until the Angel intervened. Mothers of families, large or small, can find a model of the perfect mother. No other children were needed when the Child in the Holy Family was to become the Universal Man, the new Adam and new Head of the human race.

The young man in his teens and early adulthood, young and virile, full of energy and health, can look to another young man whose sexual powers were kept in perfect check, under control, and consecrated to God. St. Joseph is the model for young men who are seeking that perfect wife and who want to keep their courtship pure and holy. His intercessory powers for sincere virginal young men and women should be very great. Even the married man and woman, who must learn to use their powers in moderation and keep those powers under complete control, can look to the parents of the Holy Family. If the typical Christian married couple must periodically practice continence, Mary and Joseph are models of perpetual continence.

I do think that our Blessed Lady, the *ever* Virgin, will always serve as the supreme model, not only of *faith* but of *purity*. Some, forgetful of the greatness of Mary as God's mother and our spiritual mother, have actually ridiculed traditional Catholic devotion to Mary. For ages, the

Church has blessed those who would pray three Hail Marys each day to which they joined, "My Mother, keep me from mortal sin this day." While we must not think we can pray and then be foolish, we should pray as though all depended upon God and work as though all depended upon us. The same is true in our challenge to keep holy and pure in God's sight.

As a young man I was taught great devotion to Blessed Mary and to St. Joseph. To this day I remember listening to the famous Father Daniel Lord, S.J., at a summer school of Catholic Action in St. Paul, Minnesota. I remember his telling us teenagers how Mary became the Mother of our Savior when she was only a teenager. He explained some of the very points I have incorporated into this chapter. Today, years later, I still turn to our Lady each day with those three Hail Marys and "My Mother, keep me from mortal sin this day (night)." I know there are thousands of other young people who have advanced into adulthood carrying the Rosary of our Lady in their pocket or purse, the scapular of Mary around their neck. I began these practices of the daily Rosary and wearing Mary's scapular around my neck when I was a boy. Today, years later, after advising thousands of modern teenagers and young adults, I still as a Catholic priest continue to carry and pray the Rosary and wear the scapular.

A few weeks before writing this chapter, I was a featured speaker in another state at its annual Marian Congress. It consisted of two days of intensive prayer and study on the Mother of God. I was impressed with the large number of young

people present, some having come from Canada.
One young engaged couple present were to be
married the following week. I expressed to them
my edification that they would come to a Marian
Congress just one week before marriage. They replied that their only regret was that the Congress
was not a week later so that they could have at-
tended during their honeymoon. It seems to this
writer, that too often, we tend to underestimate
the goodness of our young people, the faith response of which they are capable and actually
make when presented with the truth and beauty
of our holy faith in its entirety and as it applies to
the holiness of matrimony and family life.

I find it significant that the family life of our
divine Lord is largely hidden until approximately
the age of 30. Only one time do the inspired writers of sacred Scripture lift the veil on the long hidden years of the lives of Jesus, Mary and Joseph.
It was when Jesus was ending His years of childhood and first entering those transitional years of
adolescence. St. Luke carefully records it for us in
the Gospel. Obviously Mary related the incident
to Luke years later. The account is of Mary and
Joseph having to return to Jerusalem after a day's
journey when they discovered that Jesus had remained behind.

Young people now are no different than
young people in the days of our Lord's life upon
earth. They like to be often with other young people. In making the journey by primitive means,
people would walk in groups, younger people together and older people in another group where
they could discuss their points of interest as they
walked along. Pilgrimages were made in village

parties. Men and women traveling apart made it possible for the children to join either party, with their fathers or mothers. They could run back and forth. This explains why it was evening before Mary and Joseph discovered the absence of Jesus. When they came for the evening rest, families would reunite. Mary and Joseph then discovered that Jesus was absent. They looked for Him among their relatives and acquaintances.

We are informed that Jesus behaved as an ordinary boy. The response of the youthful Jesus to Mary, however, is evidence that even at the age of 12, Jesus is conscious of His divine Sonship, a thing that will be confirmed from heaven in Luke 3:22. The divinity of Jesus was to Mary as to us today, an object of faith and not vision. "What reason had you to *search* for me? Could you not tell that I must needs be in the place that belongs to my Father?" The emphasis is on *search*. Luke is pointing out here that the real and only Father of Jesus is God the Father. Luke continues and ends his narrative with emphasis on the reality of Jesus' human nature. "Jesus made progress in wisdom and stature and favor with God and men." Although Jesus had the fullness of grace from the beginning of His Incarnation, He still advanced in life humanly by growing in human wisdom as human knowledge was gained by human experience. Jesus was true God but also fully human.

A point of the Gospel I think is too often skimmed over lightly is that sentence of Luke in the final paragraph of chapter two: *"He went down with them and came to Nazareth and lived under their authority."* That sentence tells us much about the family life of Jesus. As Jesus begins the transition years (adolescence) we mentioned in Chapter V, from then until His mature adulthood, somewhere around the age of 30, we are told one thing of those long years. Joseph and Mary used their authority and Jesus was subject to them. How significant that the divinely inspired pages of sacred Scripture open for us to give us this picture of the Holy Family just when Jesus is entering those most challenging years of life. There is a deep message here for adolescents and for parents.

Mary and Joseph were surely aware of the uniqueness of their Child. The Holy Spirit overshadowed Mary. Joseph knew that he was not Christ's physical father, as he too was informed from heaven of the supernatural origin of his foster Son. It is always easier for parents to be permissive and not implement loving authority. Mary and Joseph could have had an easy excuse. But they used their authority. Else how could Jesus have been obedient to them during his adolescent years?

This incident recorded in the Bible informs us that every year the parents of Jesus went on religious pilgrimage, they had family ties with relatives, they used their authority. If they traveled on pilgrimage annually, they obviously worshipped each week at the local temple. The parents of Jesus were deeply concerned about their Child. Concern is another word for love. Besides the time required to make the pilgrimage, the fact that Jesus remained behind and Mary and Joseph had to travel back a day's journey meant two extra days in traveling.

Mary and Joseph could have said, "He's almost 13 now. He should know better and he can find his own way home." How many parents have gone looking for their teenager who was not home on time? How many have placed phone calls inquiring? How many teenagers have resented such concern of parents? How many have grown into adulthood realizing that where parents were permissive, love was not strong, and where parents were concerned and at times restrictive, love was intense.

The Holy Family of Nazareth is the supreme model of family life. All the qualities of family life and faith shine brightly and intensely and are realized ideally. Love itself became incarnate through the cooperation of Mary and Joseph. The God of the Universe becomes one of us in a family setting. There is human growth, understanding, compassion, work, suffering, faith, love, humility, kindness, gratitude, meekness, patience, mercy. The absence of the use of sexual powers does *not* point to any evil in the average marriage. Rather it reminds us that sex, in reality, is not the chief aspect of marriage. It is but one expression of all those other qualities of the sanctity of family life which Jesus, Mary and Joseph personified in perfection.

In their national Pastoral Letter on Mary, "Behold Your Mother, Woman of Faith," our American Bishops mention evils threatening and destroying human life today. The bishops have looked with special affection at "the offering of the bride's bouquet at our Lady's statue" as an American Catholic custom "that invites the Blessed Virgin into the life of the newlyweds."

Some such custom on the day of one's marriage, properly understood and appreciated, could be the beginning of the couple's consecrated married love *in Christ* looking to the Holy Family for their model and inspiration.

How beautiful is the custom of those who combine the bride's bouquet custom, recommended and praised by our bishops, with that of the Candle ceremony. There is the large candle, preferably placed before the image of the Mother of the total Christian family. It may be very ornate, specially decorated for the occasion and to last for years to come. Two smaller candles burn beside the large Christ candle before the wedding. After their marriage vows, the new husband and wife go to the image of the Mother of God where the two smaller candles burn, representing their individual lives. They now light the large single candle, bride and groom acting as one, taking the fire of the smaller candles to place the flame of their love in Christ to the large candle. They then extinguish the smaller candles and the ceremony continues with one large candle now ablaze and representing their union in Christ through the sacrament of matrimony.

I like to recommend that prospective brides and grooms adopt this custom on their wedding day. Each year thereafter, on the anniversary of their wedding, they can get out the large candle, light it anew. At this time they *renew* their marriage vows. Some home para-liturgical ceremony could be devised by husband and wife. It could be witnessed in time as the years go on by growing children. How beautiful if young children could celebrate with mother and father their wedding anniversary and witness their parents renewing their marriage vows and their love in Christ.

QUESTIONS FOR DISCUSSION

1. Explain how "triumphalism" can be both a bad spirit and *rightly balanced*, a good spirit for a Catholic Christian.
2. Should we ever apologize for our position in faith and morals as Catholics?
   a) Should we ever water down what we believe is authentic faith?
3. Explain how doctrines of faith or morals are really truths about the Person of Jesus Christ.
4. Briefly describe sanctifying grace from a biblical and ecclesiastical view.
5. What is the *key* to success in handling one's sexual powers as God intended? Explain.
6. Who is the perfect model of unselfishness and generosity as the perfect Christian? Explain.
7. Explain the role of St. Joseph in the Holy Family.
8. Was Jesus a normal child, adolescent, and young man in the minds of his contemporaries? Explain.
9. Explain: "Pray as though all depended upon God and work as though all depended upon us."
10. Give what you consider to be a truly Catholic and Christian outlook for a young engaged couple regarding the sacred powers of sex.
11. What significance can be seen in the long hidden years of our Lord's life upon earth with only a brief lifting of the veil to our view?
    a) Why does this incident, described in this

chapter, tell us much about what our family life should be like?

12. Name some customs a young bride and groom could initiate on their wedding day that could be a means of reminding them of their wedding vows and the sanctity of marriage throughout their married years.

13. Describe what you would consider the *ideal* modern Christian family.

CHAPTER XI

THE 'BIG DAY' IS FOR A
'LIFE TIME' OF ADULT LOVE

(Practical aspects in preparing for marriage)

In their document, *Basic Teachings for Catholic Religious Education,* our American bishops said: "Christ raised marriage of the baptized to the dignity of a sacrament. The spouses, expressing their personal and irrevocable consent, are the ministers of the sacrament. Therefore, they live together in Christ's grace. They imitate — and in a way represent — Christ's own love for his Church. By this sacrament Christian spouses are, as it were, consecrated to uphold the dignity of matrimony and to carry out its duties. It should be made clear that the Church discourages the contracting of mixed marriages in order to encourage a full union of mind and life in matrimony. . . .

"The special characteristic of Christian moral teaching is its total relationship to the love of God, or charity. All commandments and norms for this moral teaching are summed up in faith working through charity. Love of God is the soul of morality. God is love, and in God's plan that love reaches out in Jesus Christ, to unite men in mutual love.

"It follows then, that responding freely and perfectly to God and God's Will means keeping His commandments and living in His love. It means accepting and practicing the 'new commandment' of charity.

"Sustained by faith, man is to live a life of love of God and of his fellow men. This is his greatest responsibility, and the source of his greatest dignity. A man's holiness, whatever his vocation or state of life may be, is the perfection of love of God."

The above pertains to any state of life, but has special significance within the community of love which is the family. A considerable number of young people are not aware of the practical aspects of arranging for the wedding day. Of course, the priest must keep in mind that the wedding day is the "big day" for this particular couple, no matter how many weddings the priest has arranged for. It is sometimes difficult for a young couple to realize that it is not the first marriage the priest has assisted in arranging. Then too, with the growing number of mixed marriages, some young Catholics have mistakenly thought that the Church no longer requires contacting the Catholic pastor to arrange for a marriage. This would be a good time to emphasize to you young people that the Church still favors *Catholics marrying Catholics.* It may be difficult for some young people to see why. Even marriage counselors, from a natural point of view, will say the hopes for happiness and success in marriage are greater when both husband and wife profess the same religious faith. The ultimate goal in life is heaven. Husband and wife are to aid one another and their children in getting to heaven. Obviously this is facilitated when both are united in their minds as to the plan of God in our pilgrimage.

In the case of mixed marriages, a *dispensation* must be sought from the bishop through one's pastor. The Catholic must promise that he will do all in his power to educate the children, *both* boys and girls, in the holy Catholic faith. Obviously, if we really believe that the Catholic Church represents the fullness of true faith, our conscience will guide us in doing all we can to share this faith with our children.

Normally where one or both partners are Catholics, the marriage must be witnessed by a duly authorized Catholic priest. For a Catholic to attempt marriage without in any way seeking the assistance of the Church, is to enter an *invalid* marriage. Jesus said to His Church, "Whatsoever you bind upon earth shall be bound in heaven" (Mt. 16:19). Heaven respects the laws which the Church makes and heaven holds us to them. A Catholic must have his marriage witnessed by a Catholic priest unless dispensed from it in rare cases.

Matrimony is one sacrament the priest does *not* administer. The priest only *witnesses* the marriage. The man and woman administer the sacrament of matrimony *to each other*. The Church has said, even though heaven holds us bound, a man and a woman can validly administer matrimony and exchange their marriage vows, normally only in the presence of an authorized priest and at least two other witnesses. Since the priest, with the powers of Holy Orders which bestows the indelible character (mark) of Christ on the soul, is not needed for matrimony *essentially,* as he is for other sacraments (i.e. the Holy Eucharist, Penance, Anointing of the Sick, or Confirmation), the Church may grant a *dispensation* in *rare* cases for a Catholic to be married without the presence of a priest. There must be serious pastoral reasons and the dispensation must be granted by the Catholic bishop of the diocese, not by a parish priest. Even when this dispensation is granted, the Catholic must still have promised in writing to do all he can to have all children baptized and educated solely in the Catholic faith.

Some years ago a misunderstanding swept across the land when it was announced that in some dioceses the non-Catholic partner in a mixed marriage would no longer have to sign the promises to bring all the children up Catholic. Some mistakenly interpreted this to mean the Church was no longer concerned about which religion children were baptized or educated in. They missed this crucial point. While the non-Catholic in these dioceses would not be required to sign these promises, the total burden would now fall upon the Catholic partner to elicit the promises from the non-Catholic. Really, I think this is more realistic than the signing before a priest while the Catholic party silently observed it all.

Years ago many Catholic pastors painfully and frequently went through this ordeal. A young couple of mixed religions came to the rectory. Too often the Catholic party had not explained the promises to the non-Catholic Christian party. He left that to the priest. It became a big debate, sometimes amidst tears and resentment, between the priest and the party not Catholic. The Church appeared unreasonable, dictatorial. Admittedly, there were thousands of cases where this did not happen, and where the spouse of another Christian faith cooperated beautifully, not only before the marriage, but even in the years of the children's upbringing. But the point is, a signed statement, filed away, did not in itself do the work of educating future children in the Catholic faith. The burden to see that it is done must fall upon the Catholic partner.

Now when a couple comes hoping to enter a mixed marriage, the Catholic partner must take total responsibility for having reached an agreement with the other partner. To give an example. Shortly after the Church no longer required the non-Catholic to sign the promises, a young couple came to me. The young lady, not a Catholic, apparently with many difficulties and conflicts, turned on me because future children were supposed to be baptized and educated in the Catholic faith. I had never met her before. There was nothing personal between us. I became the symbol of her conflict. I was placed on the carpet and asked to justify why I was demanding that any future children be baptized and educated solely in the Catholic faith.

This is how I answered. "I am not making that command. In fact I have neither requested that you make that promise nor have I asked that the marriage take place in the Catholic Church." I then turned to the Catholic man and asked if he had made such a request of his fiance. He answered, "Yes." My question, "But why? Tell this young lady whom you love why you have made that request." Admittedly, I had a little anxiety over how the young man would respond. But I felt this way. The future happiness in Christ of this young couple and their future family will depend upon their working out the difficulties. I will not be living in their home. I will not be there to implement the decisions or promises. Neither will any bishop or pope.

The young man replied: "I believe the Catholic Church was founded by Jesus Christ. I believe that it has the true faith. While I respect other Christian Churches, in conscience, I just could never agree to have any of my children baptized or educated in another Church. I love my faith. I believe in it with all my heart. The only way I could be happy in this world and, I believe, in the next, is if I do all that I can to bring my children up in the Catholic faith." I turned to the young lady and responded, "Your conflict is not with me but with this young man. What is needed here is for the two of you to have further communication and reconciliation." The young lady responded, "What about my conscience?" I answered, "I respect your conscience. If you are to live in peace and harmony, you should not go contrary to your conscience. I do not advise that you make any promises in which you are not sincere and with which you could not live. I shall be happy to be of whatever assistance I can. I do believe that the two of you should spend some time alone reconciling your differences."

The young couple finally were able to recon-

cile their differences. They were married by a
Catholic priest. There developed no problems
after the marriage regarding children or the practice of the faith by the Catholic husband. But
what if they could *not* reconcile their differences?
In that case, the only answer seems that *this* couple are not meant by God for marriage to each
other. That may seem cruel. But compromise is
much more cruel. Insincerity is much more cruel.
It is dishonest. How could one have a happy marriage living with a guilty conscience, without
peace? Happiness can never be found in attempting to live a lie. The sincere and informed Catholic knows in his conscience that he must do all in
his power to educate and form all his children in
the fullness of true Catholic faith.

God gave us intellects and free wills to be
used reasonably and fairly. It is neither reasonable nor fair for two young people to permit themselves to fall into love without any precautions or
knowledge of the complications that could result.
There are many things for a couple attracted toward each other to consider *before* they encourage
the continued courtship of each other. It is said
that when one gets married, he marries not only a
single person, but sometimes a whole tribe. There
are the families of both parties to take into account. There may be cultural differences, religious differences, any number of differences that
a couple may discover they could never surmount
or reconcile satisfactorily. They have to consider
not only their own lives, but the future lives of
children and the happiness or unhappiness that
may result in the lives of children.

Surely, no young person has any right to date

anyone whom he knows he could never, in good conscience, marry. Perhaps the other partner is a divorced party not free to enter into a valid marriage in the eyes of God. There may be other reasons for not continuing to date a person with whom one discovers he has irreconcilable differences. Young couples should get to know such basic needs and differences early, before any courtship becomes so serious that emotional crises may develop that are beyond the power of the couple to handle. This is being fair and reasonable to each other and a future family. It is being honest with God and self.

Young people, in most cases, you have only one chance at marriage. *You cannot afford to make a mistake.* Parents have picked up the pieces of mistakes you may have made in preadolescent and pre-adult years, but in this one, marriage, you must be prepared and it must be *in Christ* that you find happiness in time and in eternity. Seeking a marriage partner has consequences reaching into eternity.

Many mixed marriages have worked out beautifully. Many such marriages have not. I have had Catholic young people say to me, "Well, I know of some non-Catholics that would make better husbands and wives than some Catholics." I answer, "So do I. I agree. Just because a young man and woman are of the same faith does not mean they are necessarily meant for each other for marriage. It takes more than that. This is why we must consider the *total* person, his background, mental disposition. This is why each one must get to know the other party so well that he has at least this much conviction before any serious courtship or any commitment of engagement develops. He must be convinced that both are compatible emotionally, mentally, culturally as well as religiously, that both have a common foundation of love and understanding upon which they can continue to build for life."

I've discovered unfortunate situations only after it was too late. A Catholic young lady spending her senior year in high school or final year in college dating a divorced man may come to the knowledge of the priest only when the priest is approached to perform the ceremony. How can he? The first marriage was valid. Baptized Christians of other faiths are as truly married until death as are Catholics. If the priest attempted to witness the marriage of someone already validly married, that second marriage would be no true marriage. The priest would be guilty of sin by pretending. The young lady did serious wrong by allowing herself to become involved with someone she knew she could never marry in the eyes of God and His Church. If the parents knew of the situation and did not strongly advise against it, they too share the guilt. This brings us back to the fact that God made us free, intellectual beings. If we do not use these powers properly, if we abuse them, we are responsible before God.

As indicated above the fact that both are supposedly Catholic does not always guarantee a successful marriage. There are people who call themselves Catholics, wear the label, but do not accept the fullness of Catholic faith and morals. It appears today that even some Catholics play the "conscience game." The sincere Catholic must check out even the faith of one who calls himself a

"Catholic." It is important to see that the couple have a common, wholesome, Christian outlook on married love and the upbringing of a family in Christ.

Marriage at too early an age will often spell disaster. Statistics show that, generally, about 50 percent of teenage marriages end in divorce within two years after the marriage. Some surveys indicate as high as 90% end in failure when both husband and wife marry in their teens. The chances for success are a little better if only the girl is in her teens. Of course *every* young couple desirous of marriage is convinced, even when the odds are stacked against them, that their case is different.

Sometimes it is difficult for parents, perhaps even for priests and religious, to think clearly when a young couple appear so wholesome, so much in love, that they want to get married. I once heard from a good teaching Sister who was very popular and effective in many ways with youth. She had been reading articles I'd written for some years. She had been agreeing with my approach in general. She wrote to ask me, at that time, to write a good stiff article concerning priests who would not cooperate when young people in their teens came to the Church to be married. She was convinced that their lack of sympathy, compassion, was driving some of these young people to marry out of the Church and perhaps causing them to lose their faith altogether, or at least, make them live in sin. She wanted me to write an article defending the cause of such young Catholics who wanted to marry in their teens.

The good Sister told me that Catholic

teenagers of her acquaintance had gone to priests hoping to be married but instead of compassion and consideration, had met with the priests quoting statistics of how many marriages in the United States (at least one out of four, approaching one out of three) were ending in divorce among adults and how much higher the percentage was among teenagers. I was to write an article "dealing with *persons,* the flesh and blood teenagers, not cold statistics."

I replied to the concerned Sister by stating that in conscience I could *not* write such an article. Just before receiving her letter, I had been assigned to a new parish, a small *rural* parish in the Dakotas which typified communities where family life is perhaps at its best in our country. And yet, shortly after arriving in my new parish, I had already been presented with cases involving two different marriages that had taken place in that parish less than a year before. Four teenagers were involved. They were married in the Catholic Church in the presence of the Blessed Sacrament. Both marriages had already ended in divorce, less than a year later. This meant that four young lives were now ruined. All the people involved had gone their separate ways. One boy disappeared six weeks after the wedding. Another, shortly after marriage, went into service.

I learned of one of these cases when the Catholic girl came seeking an annulment so she could marry someone else. I explained to her that her case would have to go through the bishop's office, and if her first marriage was a valid sacramental marriage in the eyes of God and His Church, there could be *no* annulment. It would have to be a case of proving that the first marriage was not in fact a valid marriage. What evidence did she have to offer whereby we could present her case to the bishop's office or the matrimonial tribunal of the diocese? She had *nothing* to offer except, "it just didn't work out." The second case I discovered when the girl came to have her baby baptized, announcing that her husband had left her within a couple months after the wedding. I am aware that such cases have been multiplied thousands of times throughout the country. The only reason often presented when seeking an annulment is, "Don't you want us to be happy?"

In response to the sincere Sister who contacted me, I asked her if she had ever spent time in the rectory dealing with problem cases. Had she ever served on a matrimonial court? Had she ever dealt with young people whose marriage had broken up shortly after the ceremony? Had she ever dealt with two lovely young people apparently in love, one of whom was married previously at 17 or 19? Then one realizes that there *is* flesh and blood, *there are persons, real persons behind every one of those statistics.* Then one realizes the Church is concerned about happiness.

In guiding young people before marriage, we must not think with our hearts only, but with our intellects as well, and make sound judgments. And so I ask you young people reading this book, *now* while you have years yet ahead of you, use not only your emotions, not only your hearts, but your whole person, your whole heart and your whole mind. Determine right now that you are not going to have your lives ruined. Make up your minds that marriage is so sacred and so solemn that you are going to prepare well, take your time. You cannot afford to be mistaken in this lifelong commitment with *one* other person in Christ. Happiness is not found by adolescents attempting adult love.

Unfortunately, there is much false thinking circulating today, even among some Catholics, which would try to declare valid marriages ended because, as they say, "the marriage is psychologically dead." The Church, however, holds to Christ's own words regarding marriage. "What God has joined together, let no man put asunder." Marriage lasts until the physical death of one of the partners.

The difference between your emotional and mental outlook on the world between the ages of 17 and 21 is vast. Even between the ages of 21 and 30 the change in outlook is considerable. Maturity comes with experience, evaluating knowledge gained in the light of experience to come to mature judgments. Some people never mature, but in general, the teenager is in no position to make lifelong commitments of any kind, let alone matrimony.

While there is no given age when marriage is universally judged proper, surely, as an average, it would seem that the *youngest* should be during the earlier years of the second decade of one's life. This hardly seems an unreasonable goal as a minimum standard. Anything less does seem unreasonable and imprudent.

Every young couple contemplating marriage should know that a certain amount of *paper* work is involved even when both are Catholic. The Church has questionnaires to be completed. Baptismal certificates are needed when one is marrying in a parish where he was not baptized. Various affidavits are often needed. Testimonies of parents or persons well known by the young couple may be required to prove freedom for marriage. In some cases, dispensations must be sought from the bishop's office. All this takes time. There are practical and spiritual reasons behind all these requirements.

The Church is most concerned about the validity and sanctity of the young couple's marriage. This is to assure them happiness in time and eternity. Investigations are needed to prove that this couple are free to enter a true sacramental marriage. Baptism is always required before any other sacrament can be received. When a Catholic is to be married, the priest must always check in the baptismal record book where the person was baptized. This is for two reasons. First, as evidence that this person is in fact baptized. Secondly, as proof that the person was never married before. Should a person attempt a second (invalid) marriage, the request for the baptismal certificate (or looking in the baptismal records) would indicate this person has already been married. If the first spouse has died, then of course, a certificate of death would be needed as evidence of freedom to marry a second time.

There is the requirement of marriage instructions, even when both are Catholic. At least six lessons seem to be a standard requirement. If the persons attempting marriage are still in their teens, some dioceses require a special board to study the particular case and pass judgment whether this particular couple are in fact mature

enough to realize the serious responsibilities they
are undertaking. But even when the couple are of
mature age, the Church asks that special instructions be offered, reviewing the faith, especially as
it concerns the dignity and sanctity of marriage.

The proper priest to approach is one's own
pastor. Usually the marriage will take place in the
parish of the Catholic young lady. The pastor of
the young man will fill out the marriage investigation papers for the groom and send them to the
proper pastor or diocese where the marriage will
take place. All of this takes time and requires
much more work on the part of the priest than
most young couples realize. Even when both are
Catholic, the young man and woman should go to
visit their parish priests at least a couple months
before the wedding is to take place. They should
not have finalized any wedding dates or had an-
nouncements printed for the wedding date until
they have discovered that everything is possible
and in proper order with the Church and their
local pastors.

One cannot go to just any priest to arrange for
marriage. One must go to the parish within which
one is a resident. This means that if you move into
a new area, shortly after arrival you should register with the pastor of the nearest Catholic parish.
A young couple should not wait until they have
serious needs of the Church's administration for
special sacraments (baptism, confirmation,
anointing, matrimony) before making their presence known. The proper thing to do is register
soon. Your mere residence makes you a member of
the parish, not the act of registering. Some mistakenly think that if they have never withdrawn

their membership in a former parish (which may
be 200 miles away) they can travel back there
whenever they need special sacraments. They are
surprised when they are informed that the priest
in their former area now needs *delegation* from
the pastor of the new area where they now live.
This may all seem like unnecessary red tape, but
it is designed for the good of souls. Catholics at a
very young age should learn to be responsible,
take an interest in their local parish, support it as
generously as they can, not only financially but
morally and spiritually.

When things are done right and with consideration, most every priest is a willing cooperator
to make one's wedding, baptism, anointing, etc.,
as beautiful and inspiring as possible. Priests generally are willing to show special consideration to
anyone who needs them, whether active members
at the parish or not. Priests strive to be ministers
of Christ's gospel of love to everyone. At the same
time, while we know most priests are thus considerate, lay people should take care to be properly
instructed, act correctly within Christ's Mystical
Body and not throw all responsibility upon their
priests by carelessness. Good Christians help
carry each other's burdens in love.

The wedding day is only the *beginning* of a
marriage. Preparations for marriage must not
consist only of that big day when the bride and
groom appear as the focal point of attention. After
the marriage ceremony and reception, even
though a big crowd may have witnessed solemni-
ties, the hundreds of witnesses return to their
daily living and cares, the newly married couple
have only begun what is normally many long

years of faithful self-sacrifice. What a pity if an immature couple were shortsighted and prepared only for a day and not a lifetime.

Ephesians, fifth chapter, gives us a true Christian picture of the family. The family is really a little Church, sometimes called a "miniature Mystical Body." The Christian family is the universal Church in miniature. Married Christians both signify and share in the mystery of that unity and fruitful love which exists between Christ and His Church. This intimate union in Christ and the total good of the children imposes complete fidelity on each of them and explains the unbreakable oneness between them. Christ Jesus has raised this union to the dignity of a sacrament so that it clearly recalls and reflects His own unbreakable union with His Church.

Christian couples nourish and develop their marriage by undivided affection which springs from the fountain of divine love. It blends a love that is both human and divine. They must remain faithful in body and mind in both good times and in bad, and have solemnly vowed themselves to do this before Christ and His Church. By its very nature, matrimony is directed toward the procreation and education of children and it is there in fruitful love that marriage finds its crown. Only in a secondary way have this man and woman invited each other to love in Christian marriage. It was primarily the Creator Himself Who extended the invitation to them to share and manifest in their union the very life of God Himself and gave them the example of His unbreakable love.

Normally the celebration of marriage should take place within the Mass. There are options the priest and couple may choose from regarding the Liturgy of the Word. Of supreme importance is the consent of the contracting parties, which the priest asks and receives. There is a special nuptial blessing for the bride and for the marriage covenant. Even in the case of mixed marriages, the bishop of the diocese may give permission for the celebrating of marriage within Mass, except that, according to general law, Holy Communion is not given to the non-Catholic. It would be regrettable for a Catholic to decline having a marriage not celebrated within the Sacrifice of the Mass.

It is ideal for both groom and bride to receive Holy Communion at their wedding (and even all present). In this way, their love is nourished and elevated into communion with our Lord and with one another. At their nuptial Mass, the Catholic bride and groom may receive our divine Lord in Holy Communion under both species. The receiving of our Lord under both kinds more fully manifests their new union in Christ.

God's invitation to marriage is a call to *adult* love. Married love, therefore, differs from the love between parents and children. A child is not expected to make major decisions, always to have control of emotions or to recognize the deeper values and principles of Christian life and love. The child sees the parent as the giver of things and the child does not have anything of comparable value to return. Really, the only thing the good parent desires is the child's love.

The adult love to which God calls married people is for two people to trust each other completely. On their wedding day, they say to each other: "We trust each other to respect each other's

168 CHARITY, MORALITY, SEX AND YOUNG PEOPLE

needs, to have communications in our decisions. We will respect the consciences of each other. We will have reverence for our sexual powers. We will be forgiving of each other's failures. Our love for each other is an overflow of our love for God. In each other we will discover more fully and deeply the mystery of God's life and love. In this love we enter and in it we will grow. We will help one another get to heaven."

This love is not only for the wedding day. It is for a lifetime. The walk down the aisle on one's wedding day is a path that leads to all future years and ends in eternity.

QUESTIONS FOR DISCUSSION

1. What is meant by "irrevocable consent" as used by our bishops?
2. Give a good Christian explanation of the two words:
   a) adult
   b) love
3. In the Catholic Church, mixed marriages are allowed only with a special dispensation from the bishop. Explain why the Church discourages marriages between persons of different faiths, even though both are Christian.
4. State the laws of the Church regarding marriage.
5. A Catholic attempts marriage without going to see a priest for obtaining necessary dispensations and is married outside the Catholic Church. Does the Church consider this marriage valid before God?
6. Normally, how should the marriage of a Catholic take place?

7. Summarize the things necessary for a young couple contemplating marriage in regard to their arrangements with the Church before marriage.

8. In the case of a mixed marriage, what must the Catholic promise with regard to the baptism and education of the children?

9. Explain: "No young person has a right to date anyone whom he knows he could never marry in good conscience."

10. What does the record say about teenage marriages?

11. Explain: "Behind those statistics are real persons."

12. Explain: "One's emotional and mental outlook on the world and fellow man during the teens and the maturity of adulthood differs considerably."

13. Who is the proper priest to approach in arranging for marriage?

14. A couple are arranging for a mixed marriage. The Catholic boy thinks, "such things are for the girl to take the lead." She takes him to see her minister. The minister, who may be very sincere, announces that the Catholic Church no longer requires the assistance of the priest so there is no need to see the priest before the marriage. Is this correct? Should the Catholic boy first have gone to see his Catholic pastor?

15. Explain: The prospective couple are preparing not simply for a wedding day but for a lifetime of *adult married love*.

16. Explain why it is ideal to be married within the Catholic Mass.

CONCLUSION:
MARRIAGE IS GOD'S CALL

In this book I have attempted to bring together the elements of charity, morality and sex
as it pertains to you. I think it essential that all
the elements of faith be considered in any book
that pretends to include sex education. Where I
have failed or been deficient, I pray for your love
and your faith. I pray that God Himself will sup-
ply my deficiency. The education and formation
in the homes into which you were born will complete your preparation for adult life. Then too, the
contributions of other religious educators should
win your gratitude in Christ.

A book that offers sex education without morality, even if the education is valid, could be very
disturbing. We all have weaknesses due to the
consequences of Original Sin. A book on sex education that treats exclusively the moral aspects,
and I mean here morality that is orthodox in the
mind of the Church, could still seem legalistic and
cold, for it would not be complemented with that

fullness of Catholic Christian faith that brings warmth, tenderness and understanding to every aspect of human life.

To permit you young people to grow into physical maturity without ever having presented to you sex education according to the mind of the Catholic Church, which is the mind of Jesus Christ, would involve being guilty of serious neglect. To present authentic human love unblended with divine love or charity would be to fail to be Catholic and Christian. Perhaps all that we have attempted in this book on Charity, Morality, Sex and Young People will require more than one reading. Perhaps a year or two from now, another review of this book will bring to each of you a deeper and holier insight than was gained at this moment of your physical, mental and spiritual development. I hope the book will assist you personally and help your parents fulfill their primary obligations.

God gives a call to each one of us. He calls most of us to marriage. Marriage is *God's call* to a state for the sanctification and salvation of husband and wife. Their sanctification is obtained in their union according to the conditions established by Almighty God in His Son, Jesus Christ.

Looked at only as a *natural* contract, marriage is a mutual consent of man and woman to give to each other the right to sexual relations, and to assist one's natural needs and common interests. But for you Catholic Christian young people, marriage will be more. Christian marriage has salvific power which flows from its sacramentality. It is that which will make all aspects, even sexual relations, salvific, grace filling. You and your spouse will be God-chosen instruments in Christ's sanctifying and saving work. Your consent to marriage, blessed by the Church, will open a spiritual treasury to you and any future children. Some day you will actually administer the sacrament of matrimony to your spouse and you will have the care of each other's souls.

St. Paul under the inspiration of the Holy Spirit (Eph. 5, 23), said, "the husband is the head of the wife as Christ is the head of the Church." Boys, remember that means that the husband's first and principal purpose will be a religious one. The man must lead his wife and children in witnessing Christ in faith, in instilling trust in God and between the family members. Then the father of the family becomes like Christ who is "the Savior of his body."

Girls, God's word says that wives should so conduct themselves in the family and so honor their husbands that the wife gives him a better idea of his true dignity as chief representative of Christ in the home. The wife must manage everyday activities of the family in such a manner that they contribute toward the salvation of husband and any children they may have. If the husband is the head of the home, the wife is the heart, and both are in a position of authority over their children in the name of Christ Jesus.

Love is the soul of morality. Faith is the substance of things to be hoped for. Human sexuality is a power that reflects God the Creator. It is a power God uses, a power with which men cooperate to manifest human love and divine love. It is a power God uses, through us, to create souls made in His image and likeness, destined for heaven.

QUESTIONS FOR DISCUSSION

1. What is meant by human love blending with divine love!
2. God's call to marriage is not only a call to rear children but a call to two people's sanctification and salvation. Discuss.
3. Explain: "Christian marriage has salvific power which flows from its sacramentality."
4. What is the first and principal role of the husband?
5. What is the supporting role of the wife in the family?
6. Explain: "Love is the soul of morality."

TO SETTLE YOUR CONSCIENCE
by Rev. Cass Kucharek

TO SETTLE YOUR CONSCIENCE is Reverend Cass Kucharek's sensible, layman's guide to moral theology. Its sole aim is to be practical in solving the moral problems of everyday life. Using solid Catholic reasoning together with realistic examples, TO SETTLE YOUR CONSCIENCE brings peace to the mind and soul by defining exactly the Church's position on individual acts. TO SETTLE YOUR CONSCIENCE could provide the answer you've been looking for. 262 pages, paperbound, No. 877 . . . $3.95

THE FAITH OF MILLIONS
by Rev. John A. O'Brien, Ph.D.

A completely revitalized update of the original best-seller, THE FAITH OF MILLIONS thoroughly presents all of the historic doctrines of the Catholic faith, with insights from Vatican II . . .

> ". . . the majority of problems came from those who could not reconcile the changelessness of the pre-Vatican II Church with the changing Church of today."

THE FAITH OF MILLIONS is one book that answers the questions of all persons interested in the Catholic faith. A clear, concise reconfirmation of the Church in our time. 416 pages, paperbound, No. 830 . . . $4.95

IMITATION OF CHRIST
by Thomas à Kempis

This updated version of Thomas à Kempis' 15th century classic preserves the spirit of Christ-centered serenity that made à Kempis a sought-after spiritual mentor. For modern Christians, the IMITATION OF CHRIST

offers the inspiring picture of a life of humility, fore-
bearance and total commitment to Christ.

"The kingdom of God is within you" says the
Lord. *Focus yourself with your whole heart on the
Lord and forsake the miserable world, and your
soul shall find rest.*

Translated from the original Latin and rendered into
modern English by Albert J. Nevins, M.M.; the *IMITA-
TION OF CHRIST* contains four books, 114 chapters,
36 picture "thought starters" and comes in a 224 page
pocket-sized edition. Paperbound, No. 778 . . . $1.50

PORTRAITS OF FAITH
by Father Clifford Stevens

Catholic history is constantly uncovering the forgotten
histories of many interesting martyrs and pioneers.
Many lived in times of turbulence and change, yet
managed to keep their balance and vision intact. Their
exciting vignettes bring to the forefront the founda-
tions of human civilization and development carved
by these long forgotten, but immensely interesting
personalities. 176 pages, paperbound, No. 764
. . . $2.25

If your bookseller does not have these titles, you may
order them by sending listed price (we pay postage
and handling) to the Book Department at the address
below. Enclose check or money order — do not send
cash.

Write for free book list

Our Sunday Visitor, Inc.
Noll Plaza
Huntington, IN 46750